SQUARE PEG

SQUARE PEG

The Life and Times of a

NORTHERN NEWSPAPERMAN

South of the Border

DENNIS KENNEDY

First published 2009

Nonsuch Publishing
119 Lower Baggot Street
Dublin 2
Ireland
www.nonsuchireland.com

British Library Cataloguing in Publication Data.
A catalogue record for this book is available from the British Library.

ISBN 978 1 8458 8968 5

Typesetting and origination by The History Press
Printed in Great Britain

Contents

One

A Bus, Not a Beanstalk

Winston Churchill once described Uganda as a fairytale in the clouds, reached, not by climbing up a beanstalk, but by a railway. Glencullen was, to me in 1970, another world, reached neither by a beanstalk nor a railway, but via the 44B bus and that year's national bank-strike in Ireland. And by way of Ethiopia, not Uganda.

Churchill, in 1907, found Uganda a wonderful new world. The scenery, he wrote, was different, the vegetation was different, the climate was different, and, most of all, the people were different. I felt much the same about Glencullen in 1970. And still did after it had been my home for twenty years.

For those who don't know it, Glencullen is in the Dublin Mountains. It would be the first of the Wicklow glens, if it was not almost entirely within the county of Dublin. It runs south-east from just above Rathfarnham, down between the Two Rock and the Glendoo and Glencullen mountains towards Enniskerry, where it joins Glencree.

The crossroads at Glencullen is barely ten miles from St Stephen's Green, but it is a thousand miles from suburbia. Glencullen is on the road to nowhere. One of the two roads that intersect at Johnny Fox's pub has got there by twisting up off the main Dublin to Enniskerry route at Stepaside, up over a shoulder of the Two Rock at Ballyedmunduff, down into Glencullen, and still further down to the Devil's Elbow, across the Glencullen River, into County Wicklow and, eventually, if you don't get lost, to Enniskerry. The other arm of the crossroads is formed by the route that straggles for three miles up the steep hill from Kilternan and runs high along the northern slope of the glen, past the village, and away up to the remote head of the glen before passing over into the Pine Forest, and from there either further up onto the Military Road, or down past the ruins of the barracks to Rathfarnham.

Like many others in Ireland, when we returned home in 1968 after some years in Ethiopia, I had never heard of Glencullen. Our first priority – my wife Katherine's and mine – was to find somewhere to live for ourselves and our two brand-new Ethiopian-born children. To give us a holiday, and also time to look, we rented a house in Malahide for two weeks in July; we stayed six months, partly because we rather liked Malahide but mainly because we had nowhere else to go.

We had nowhere else to go because any house we could afford we did not like, and any house we liked we could not afford. We had come home from abroad with grand ideas of buying a not too run-down Georgian town house for a few thousand pounds, and fixing it up. A few thousand pounds was all we had, but didn't everyone get a mortgage anyway?

There were plenty of houses roughly fitting our specification, but we soon found they were all either too run-down, or too dear. In August 1968 I started work in *The Irish Times* at a salary of about £1,600 a year, which meant that I could hope to borrow, under the rules then prevailing, at most £4,000 – two and a half times my annual salary. So our ceiling was not much above £5,000. In those days 100% mortgages were undreamed of, and you were lucky to get a loan above 75% of the value of the property. Ever optimistic, we convinced ourselves that if a house was in prime condition, needing no work done to it, we just might stretch to £7,000.

We almost did it. We found a Georgian terraced house, in good condition, going for just under the £5,000 mark. It was not in Dublin itself, but in Lucan, one of that splendid terrace of grand houses tucked behind the Spa Hotel and looking out over rear gardens sloping down to a golf course and the rolling countryside. We liked it, it almost fitted our bill, there was a good Protestant school in Lucan, and a decent bus service into the city. It met the one criterion that the bank manager friend of a friend I had first consulted on house purchase in Dublin had specified – it had off-street parking. This was 1968 remember, so he was a far-sighted bank manager.

But the house had some defects. It was reached by a rough roadway that wound round the hotel, unlighted as I recall, and overhung by trees. My wife did not fancy walking home alone on a winter evening. It also needed some work done, and it was on three levels, which would mean a lot of mountaineering with two infants less than three years of age.

We were daunted, terrified perhaps, at the idea of plunging ourselves into such vast debt. We had never bought a house. I had only recently been persuaded that we had to buy, rather than rent. I had been brought up in a rented house; I had had vaguely socialist ideas that buying a house was slightly immoral. Hadn't Proudhon said property was theft? So we were almost relieved when an estate-agent friend of the mother of a friend, hearing on the extensive Dublin grapevine that we were thinking of buying the Lucan house, sent word down the line back to us to beware of woodworm, dry rot, or rising damp, or perhaps it was all three, that he had heard were in the terrace and could run though it.

At the time we were naïve enough to assume that this twice-removed estate agent – or indeed any other estate agent – had our best interests at heart. It never occurred to us that he might have had a few houses on his own books, and that he saw a prospect of off-loading one of them onto the friends of the daughter of his friend.

So we said no to Lucan. Then we found a house in Howth. It was a bungalow high on the Hill of Howth, in not good but fair order, with a large sloping garden. It faced unfashionably north, was a good hike from Howth village, and railway station, and would need some work, but at £5,200 we could just afford it. We took the plunge and made an offer to the owner (it was a private sale). He said yes and we put the solicitors to work. Then he phoned me up and said there was a problem. Some time ago he had promised the brother-in-law first refusal if he ever sold the bungalow, but it was so long ago he had assumed he was not interested. Now the brother-in-law was mad keen to buy it, and it was all very difficult.

What he would do, to be fair all round, would be to sell it at the agreed price to whichever of us could first bring a contract ready for exchange round to his solicitor's office in Stephen's Green the following Monday morning. He told me this on the phone late on a Friday afternoon. My solicitor was a thrusting young Galway fellow I had met at student debates years earlier who had now set up in practice in Dublin. He jumped into action and spent Saturday morning with me going over all the details, and telling me not to worry, he would be at your man's office first thing on Monday and the house would be mine.

When he phoned me some time after ten on Monday morning to tell me he was just setting out to cross the Green and was I absolutely certain I wanted to go ahead with the deal, I knew I had lost it. And so I had. Even in the Dublin of 1968, 10am was not first thing in the morning. It was like a bereavement; for years we could not bear to go near that part of the Hill of Howth. Relations with my solicitor were less cordial than they had been.

Still houseless after six months in Malahide, we migrated south to Monkstown, and a fine ground-floor rented flat in an elegant Edwardian villa in Alma Road. For a few months painting walls, sanding floors, attending auctions and wrestling with small gardens front and rear, took precedence over house-hunting.

We liked Alma Road; it was right beside Seapoint railway station, and the train took me into Tara Street – Sir John Rogerson's Quay, to give it its full title in those days – very close to *The Irish Times*. Getting home was not so easy, as the last train left Amiens Street at 7pm, just when *The Irish Times* was getting busy. But the bus service was good, even if the buses were antiquated, smelly and creaking in every joint. It was on one of those buses that a minor jolt was administered to my romantic ideas of Ireland and Irishness.

Going in to town one sunny summer morning on a double-decker bus, I was sitting downstairs on that odd seat at the front which ran along the back of the driver's cab, meaning whoever was sitting on it faced the rest of the bus. A few stops on some passengers boarded, and I found myself gazing at close quarters into one of the best known, and hairiest, faces in Ireland. It was, unmistakably, Luke Kelly of the Dubliners, then at the height of their fame, and the embodiment of rumbustious, irreverent and essential Irishness.

As I looked, he reached into his pocket and pulled out a newspaper. It was the *Daily Mirror*. I spent the rest of the journey trying to digest the fact that this most Irish of Irishmen was a devotee of that most English of tabloids. In fact, I should not have been surprised, as the *Mirror* then, and for years afterwards, sold far more copies in Dublin than did *The Irish Times*.

Alma Road was also very handy, in summer, for bathing at Seapoint, just beside the Martello Tower. Dublin Bay was said to be polluted, and one sometimes encountered odd looking artefacts in the water, but as everyone still swam in it, we did likewise. We instituted swimming lunches, when salt-water stalwarts from *The Irish Times* would come out in the train and have a swim at Seapoint followed by lunch in our tiny, partly walled garden behind the flat. Admission was strictly by presentation of a wet set of togs. Donal Foley, John Horgan, Jack Fagan, Mary Maher and an eager new recruit to the staff called Maeve Binchy were among the regulars.

Living in Monkstown meant that our house-hunting, when we resumed it, concentrated on the Southside, and we gave up ideas of living in Malahide, Howth, Sutton, or, at a pinch, in Baldoyle. Now we acquired an intimate knowledge of the coastal stretch from Sandymount to Killiney, and to this day can point out numerous houses we nearly bought. (In fact we never came near buying any of them, as by this time there was nothing on the Southside for less than £7,000.)

We were also becoming fluent in the language of the estate agent. We knew that when our auctioneer was offering a 'bijou residence', ideal for a young couple, at a price we could afford, it would be two bedrooms and a back yard; and that a house of 'great character', ideal for restoration, would be a wreck in need of complete re-building. We also discovered that desirable districts, such as Ballsbridge, or Dalkey, had elastic boundaries.

So we ventured inland and explored Glenageary, Leopardstown and Cabinteeley. We were tempted by a restored cottage out near Lucan, in beautiful condition, carpeted from end to end in Tintawn, and being sold by a gentleman who had helped steal the Lane Pictures from the Tate Galley in London in the 1950s. But even the vendor's noble national record was not enough to make us buy when we heard that most of the surrounding countryside was about to be bought for housing. And so it was. Then we looked at a house in Bray, in that terrace down by the sea where James Joyce once lived. But it was too far out, or too run-down, or too dear, or all three.

After a year in Monkstown, with house prices rising at a rate that bore no relationship whatsoever to journalistic salaries, we decided we just had to find somewhere. The obvious solution was to go for an estate house. We had thought of this during our north-side sojourn, and had looked at the new Bayside. But to me, that was admitting defeat, and anyway, having grown up in a very modest three-bed semi, I was too ambitious, or too much of a snob, to settle for that. In desperation we almost opted for Ballinclea Heights, in Killiney, then at the better end of estate development, and just about within our reach.

By this time half my colleagues in *The Irish Times*, and numerous old friends from my wife's earlier days in Dublin, were almost as frantic as we were to find us a house. Suggestions and addresses rained in from all sides. We should buy a site and build on it. A firm out in Leixlip was selling ready-made log cabin houses, all fitted and kitted, and you could put one of them on a neat site. We went out to Leixlip to look, and liked what we saw. We went as far as going to the auction of a site on the sea front at Sutton, ready to bid, but it was far beyond our means. Then we heard of one of these log cabins on a beautiful site on the far side of Enniskerry – we were expanding our horizons by now.

We were captivated, and despite distance, worries about bus services, snow in winter and allied concerns, we decided to bid. I was out of the country, so my wife, accompanied by our late-rising solicitor, went to the auction. Again, we were not in the running. We swore we would never go to another auction. That severely limited our options, as almost all property in Dublin was, then as now, sold at auction. What we should do, said another friend, was buy a derelict cottage in the country and rebuild it. That was what everyone was doing now, he assured us.

At that juncture another colleague, a single lady who had long been searching for a rural retreat, told me she knew of just such a cottage. Friends had told her of this particular one, but, having seen it, she thought it was not what she wanted. But we might like to look at it.

It was in Glencullen.

Two

Initiative, Imagination, and a Bank Strike

We set out to find Glencullen on a pelting-wet Saturday in March 1970. With our two young children aboard our trendy two-tone (second-hand) Triumph Herald, we followed the directions; out towards Enniskerry, through Stepaside to Kilternan, and after the second church, not the Protestant stone one with the steeple, but the pale-blue Catholic wooden one with the statue of the Virgin, took the first right and continued up the hill for most of three miles till we reached Fox's pub, then we turned left, and round a sharp bend to the right when we should have seen the cottage.

But we saw no cottage. The road plunged down to a precipitous hairpin bend and across a narrow bridge. Not having any idea where we were or where we were going, we turned in a gateway and went slowly back up the hill. In the slanting rain I would have missed it again, but my wife insisted she saw something behind the high hedge on the right. We stopped and trudged back; she was right, there was a cottage crouched up against the hedge, its back to the road, and set below the level of the road. There was no 'For Sale' sign to be seen, but it looked deserted, so we pushed our way in through a gateway overgrown by bushes.

For Sale: Lil Doyle's Cottage, April 1970. 'Wouldn't give a thousand for it.'

It was not love at first sight. The cottage was a sorry-looking affair. It had a slate roof, and walls from which plaster of a sort was peeling, revealing bits of crumbling granite. It had a lean-to porch at the front, and a couple of outhouses marching down the hill from the lower gable. It sat on a long narrow site, cut off from the road by the tall thorn hedge, and from the field sloping away from its front by a large sycamore and another high hedge. It was not possible to see much through its three small windows, but it seemed furnished.

I think we both added it mentally to our rejected list. But we had found Glencullen, so we explored a bit further. On a wet winter's day it certainly was bleak, but it was also romantically wild, and unbelievably remote though less than half an hour's drive from the advanced civilisation of Monkstown. We came back a few days later, when the sun was trying to shine, and drove up the road along the shoulder of the glen towards the Pine Forest, and back down again, marvelling at the beauty of the place.

Far up the glen we noticed the ruins of an old cottage in a field by the roadside, no more than the foundations of a stone wall or two and a bit of a gable, but with a breath-taking view. This was what we needed – enough of a ruin to make planning permission possible, but not enough to make it worth more than we could pay.

I spent the next week trying to find out who owned the ruin. No one knew, or at least no one wanted to tell me. The nearest I got was that it belonged to someone who had emigrated years ago, and it was not at all clear who held the title to it. I realised I was wasting my time, but I was not giving up on Glencullen. We went back to look at the first cottage; with no rain and a bit of winter sunshine it didn't look so bad. And it had a magnificent panoramic view down Glencullen and across to the Sugar Loaf, or it did when you peered through the dense hedge that hemmed it into its narrow site.

We asked about it locally, and were told it was Lil Doyle's cottage, and had been unoccupied since she had died a year or two earlier. They believed it might be for sale, and we should go and see Jack Flanagan, the relative who, they believed, now owned it. Jack Flanagan lived in the old forge, at the top of the hill above Lil Doyle's. When I tracked him down I found the old forge was, if anything, in a worse condition than Lil Doyle's. It was certainly smaller, darker, and sat gable-end onto the road. Jack himself seemed in fairly poor repair, but he was straight enough about the cottage. Yes he was thinking of selling it, and the price was £3,500. No there was no agent involved, but he would have to clear it with another relative who had some claim to it. I could have a look at it if I wanted.

I arranged to come back the following day with Katherine. Jack gave us a large key and told us to take our time and have a good look round. It was spooky. The small porch led into the middle room of three. With the door closed the only light came in through one small window at the front, but it was enough to see that the room reached up to the slates. There was a big basket fire place, overhung by cooking irons. A cup dangled from a hook on a rickety dresser. An old couch sat alongside a wooden staircase that ran up along the back wall to a tiny sleeping room above the fire place, a room with a ceiling so low that we had to crouch in it.

To the left of the main room was a bedroom, which had a high double bed, with chamber pot and a pair of shoes under it, and a dressing table still strewn with jars and hair brushes. On a peg behind the door hung an old-fashioned dressing gown. The wall on the other side of the centre room was a wooden partition that stretched up to the pitched roof. There was one door at floor level, and another, incongruously, just above head height, but with no visible means of ascent. (We were told later that the room behind it had been used as a granary.) We pushed open the lower door, to find an even darker room, with nothing in it. Nothing, that is, except woodworm, for our first steps took us through the floorboards and we soon saw that most of the floor had been eaten away. The same was true of the furniture in the other rooms, and of the staircase we had blithely gone up.

Against the front wall of the middle room there was a large white sink with one cold water tap. It worked, and was the only running water in the cottage, apart from that which had clearly come down through the slate roof. There was also electricity, with one light bulb still working. There was no bathroom, nor any sign of an outside lavatory.

Attached to the lower gable was an outhouse that we could see had once been a cottage in its own right, even smaller than the main one, but was now just a one-room shack. Stuck on to its gable was a lean-to shed, with granite troughs in it that suggested it had once been a piggery. Below that the narrow site disappeared into brambles and nettles.

Not even our auctioneer, in his most optimistic mode, could have attached the word 'bijou' to it, though he might have insisted it had character and a lot of potential. To us it seemed a mess, and a very remote one at that. But we were desperate, and this was the first property that we had seen that we could probably afford to buy, that we could so do without going to an auction, without dealing with an estate agent, and without, as far as we knew, competing with another buyer. And there was that magnificent view.

We returned the key and said we would think about it. For the next few days I thought about little else, and then I made the fatal mistake of drawing rough plans of how we might adapt and modernise the cottage. (I was an architect *manqué*.) I assumed we could buy it and make it habitable all within our limit of, at most, £7,000, and I also assumed I would be able to borrow enough on a building society mortgage.

So we went back and had another look. Jack said if we bought it we could have the contents too, which sounded great until you actually looked at them. But it was another plus; there was a good old mahogany table, too tough for the feasting woodworm, a Victorian wall clock, and in the loft sleeping area a large framed print of the Volunteers at College Green. I fancied that. There were some books; one was *The R.E.P. (Rubbing Eases Pain) Book,* which suggested a previous occupant had suffered from the damp.

By now I was excited at the prospect, but not too carried away that I was going to rush into it without some expert advice. A friend in the office had a cousin who was a builder, who, he was sure, would have a look at the cottage and set me straight on the whole thing. So I arranged a visit, and we drove in convoy up to Glencullen. It was now April, and, as can happen, winter had returned. A light covering of snow lay on frosty ground. The massive hedges along the road and between the cottage and the field had been savagely trimmed, leaving it cruelly exposed, and even more bleak than before.

I opened the door and my somewhat taciturn builder man strode in. He poked here and there, sniffed a lot, banged his head when he tried to stand up in the loft, muttered a warning about the state of the stairs, and breathed heavily when he saw the gaps in the floor of the empty room.

Still without expressing an opinion he suggested we go outside and have a look at the roof. So we pushed our way up the through the brambles to the top of the narrowing site from where we could look back at eye-level with the roof. He studied the slates, patched here and there with bits of cement, sighed, and turned to me.

'What's he asking?'

'£3,500,' I replied.

'Wouldn't give a thousand for it.'

And with that my builder of few words stomped off to his car and drove away. I stood gazing at the forlorn cottage in a bleak landscape, and in a mixture of frustration and anger, I think I decided at that moment that I would buy it anyway.

The next day I called in at the old forge and asked Jack what he really wanted for the cottage, adding that my expert advice was that it was not worth a thousand. He smiled gently and said he knew fine well he could get far more than he was asking if he put it properly on the market. We haggled a bit more, and in the end he said he would knock £250 off. So I settled and wrote him a cheque for £50 as a deposit. He said that was fine, he would not sell to anyone else. The deal was done.

All I had to do now was tell Katherine I had bought a ruin worth less than a thousand and paid three times that for it; and that someone had been in the house and helped himself to some of the contents; my Volunteers print was gone, but the mahogany table was still there. And also, of course, I had to find the money to pay the balance and the cost of restoration.

I had never bought a house before, but had been assured there was nothing to it. You just went to a building society and they gave you the money. The gentlemen of the Educational Building Society and *The Irish Times* shared the Pearl Bar in Fleet Street, and a preliminary unofficial consultation there told me I would need to have some plans and an estimate for the rebuilding. An architect friend of a friend agreed to draw a plan and keep an eye on the building. His plans looked good; the roof was so far gone, he said, that we would have to put on a completely new one, and if we were doing that we should raise it by four feet, leaving room for a full first floor into which he could fit a bathroom and three bedrooms. The new upper walls could be rendered and painted white, and would blend in well with the original granite of the existing walls. So we applied for planning permission, and he got in a few estimates from builders, which suggested I could refurbish the cottage for just about £4,000.

Yes, said the building society, that looks great. Come back and see us when the work is finished and we will be happy to give you a mortgage. But how do I get the work done without the money? Go and see your bank manager.

Bank managers in those days had names and faces, and you could go and see them and have a cup of tea. Mr Franklin at the Provincial in College Street was very forthcoming with tea, biscuits and advice. Sounds great, he said, but we could not authorise a loan just like that; you would have to borrow from our finance company, not from us. So, armed with his best wishes and an introduction, off I went to the finance company, who said no, the Department of Finance rules currently in force meant they could lend only for 'productive purposes'. My argument that rebuilding a house was very productive cut no ice.

Time was passing, and I was not sure which disaster I feared most – that Jack Flanagan would get tired waiting and sell the cottage to someone else, or that I would be left the penniless, and homeless, owner of a wreck which I could never afford to repair. So I blew all my savings and paid Jack the balance. I also told the architect to accept the estimate one builder had submitted for about £4,000.

Then it was back to Mr Franklin at the Provincial. He heard me out, asked me a bit more about my plans, noted my determination (actually it was desperation), looked me in the eye and remarked 'Mr Kennedy, you have great initiative and imagination. Two great handicaps in this country, I'm afraid.' My only hope, he said, was to get a bridging loan from a private bank, where you could always get money, but it would cost the proverbial arm and leg.

As before, the Pearl Bar provided the connection. One of the regulars there was on the board of the Lombard, and through him I made contact. I would need a proper valuation of the cottage, I was told, before they could consider any loan. OK, I said.

Then the banks went on strike. The stoppage that began on 30 April 1970 was teetotal. The bank doors were closed, no money went in or out, cheques were neither lodged nor debited.

Planning permission for Glencullen had just come through, and the builder, a Mr McD, had indicated that he could make a start in a month or so, and if he did, he would probably finish the job by October, if not September. What was I to do? The vision of moving into a modernised cottage, with central heating, in an idyllic mountain setting, well before winter, was irresistible. I would have a month or so before the bills would start coming in, and if the worst came to the worst, I would just have to go for the costly bridging loan.

So I told the architect to give McD the go-ahead, and the work began. Meanwhile we were all learning to live with the bank-strike. As the first weeks went by Dubliners found their own way of coping. Everyone needed money, but no one wanted to have piles of it sitting at home or in the office waiting for the burglar. The trick was to keep it in circulation. So, for us *Irish Times* workers, the Pearl Bar replaced its neighbour, the Provincial, as a banking institution.

Gus Weldon, the curate in charge, would take our salary cheques and cash them, deducting anything owing on drink consumed. Some of the cash thus put into circulation would go straight back into Mr Weldon's till, ready for further re-circulation. Supermarkets did the same; the system was built on trust – trust that the cheques being stacked up against the day when the banks reopened would indeed be honoured and anyway, it could only be a matter of days before the strike was settled.

But the strike went on; there was, as the wags put it, no danger of a settlement. At the end of July the first bill came in from my builder. He wanted £750. He would take a cheque. I did not have £750, but I could write a cheque. I wrestled with my Northern Protestant soul; should I write a cheque knowing I had no money in the bank, and hope that the bank strike went on, or should I rush round to some commercial Scrooge and beg money at whatever cost?

I wrote the cheque. The system worked smoothly; my builder took the cheque down to Mulveys' Builders Providers in Dundrum, where he received half its value in bricks, mortar and timber, and the other half in cash, which he needed to pay his workers, and which Mulveys' did not want lying around waiting to be stolen.

September 1970. Work in progress.

A month later I wrote another cheque, this time for £1,000, and this time on a cheque from a book of blanks, purchased at Easons, on which one wrote the name of one's Bank, and added a postage stamp to make it legal. This exercise was necessary as the banks were still firmly bolted, and everyone was running out of proper cheque books.

Every rumour of a settlement, or even of resumed talks, meant sleepless nights for me. As autumn approached these became more frequent, partly because my builder's promise of finishing by October was proving unrealistic. As builders do, he had taken on another job shortly after starting mine and was juggling the two of them. Besides that, the rebuilding was turning out to be more ambitious than we had first thought. When the crumbling plaster was taken off the outside walls, what was revealed was not fine cut granite, but a mixture of field stones and what the locals informed me was 'brown bread granite'. No description could have been more apt – it looked like brown bread, it crumbled in your hand like brown bread, and was every bit as porous.

Wet and windy weather would mean a halt to all work, and then, when the sun came out, our builder, and his carpenter and bricklayer, would mysteriously disappear. I was now staking everything on a two-horse race, betting that the house would be finished and I would have a mortgage before the bank strike ended. Never having bought a lottery ticket, nor entered a bookie's shop, I was ill-prepared for the sort of stress involved, and the sleepless nights increased. I had regular visions of being called to account by Mr Franklin.

After about five months the work was near enough completion to allow me to apply formally for my mortgage. At almost that precise moment in mid-November, the bank strike ended. The mortgage took until February to come through, but it took even longer for the banks to work through the backlog of cheques that had been written during the strike. My net advance cheque from the EBS for £6,131.10 must have beaten the day of reckoning at the Provincial Bank by a short head.

When the banks eventually reopened I paid a nervous first visit to College Street, wondering what I should say to Mr Franklin. Should I brave it out and thank him for the interest-free loan he had inadvertently given me as reward for my initiative and imagination, or should I say nothing and thank my lucky stars. I was spared the choice; he had reached retirement during the strike. I never saw him again.

Three

Meet the Neighbours

We moved into Glencullen in the first week of January 1971. As we did, an exceptionally mild spell gave way to real winter, and Glencullen greeted us with snow and ice. By now Lil Doyle's house had become 'Whin Cottage'; twee, I admit, but we had been obliged to come up with a name double quick in order to put in an application for a telephone. (At that time you could wait for a year for a phone.) The name was needed because the houses in Glencullen were not numbered, or at any rate the numbering did not extend to ours, as it was more than a bit of a field beyond the end of the village.

There was even some doubt as to the name of the road; the locals called it Barrack Road, because one of the cottages nearer to the crossroads had once been a police barracks. We were later told it was officially Bridge Road, but we stuck to Barrack Road. 'Whin Cottage' was chosen after we had eliminated 'Wit's End', 'The Mortgage', and similar feeble efforts at humour, partly because the cottage, and most of the hillside around it, had been smothered in whin bushes when we bought it the previous summer, and partly because whin, the northern word for gorse, was my assertion of Northernness.

Unfortunately the work of building, and clearing and extending the garden, had completely eliminated the whins from anywhere near the cottage, and we were reduced, the following spring, to transplanting some wild bushes from a neighbouring field. But the same work had given our new home a superb uninterrupted panoramic view that stretched from the Sugar Loaf right round to the distant peaks of Snowdonia. (The latter visible only on exceptionally sharp winter days, and then with the keen eyes of youth or the help of some binoculars.)

When we moved in that January we knew nothing about Glencullen, and almost no one in it. Jack Flanagan we knew, after a fashion, having bought the house from him. We had met his niece, Joan, and her husband, a namesake of mine, Tom Kennedy, who lived close by and had been employed by our builder to deliver bulk loads to the site and use his JCB to dig a septic tank and other vital excavations. We knew Johnny Cotter, a wiry little man whom we had already dubbed the Human JCB because of his prowess with the long-handled shovel, which he had been exercising on our behalf on paths and other bits of site work. We had met Joe Houlihan, the farmer from whom, after much haggling, I had bought an extra strip of field in front of the house, which I simply had to have in order to fit in the septic tank. (£240, it had cost me, plus the exchange of a valuable bit of road frontage above the cottage.)

In my dealings with all of them, they had been absolutely straight. I was a Northerner, and this was the early 1970s when the North was beginning to be really bad news. I was Protestant, at a time when Nationalist blood was up. I was a total blow-in. But no one made me feel like one. Jack Flanagan, on the strength of my £50 deposit, refused to consider offers from others eager to give him more for Lil Doyle's cottage. Joe Houlihan, who was cute enough to know that I could not make the cottage habitable without a septic tank, and that the original site was too narrow to afford the statutory distance from the public road needed for permission to sink one, had me over a barrel, and could have demanded double or treble, but didn't.

We had met Jimmy and Eleanor Tobias, delightfully eccentric cousins who had married late in life and moved into a cottage beside the Glencullen River, just over the bridge in County Wicklow. It was through them, indirectly, that we had first heard of Lil Doyle's cottage. But beyond that, we knew no one. It was not long before we did.

Sean the Postman had watched the rebuilding of the cottage, and had stopped in once or twice when I had been up inspecting progress or beginning to wrestle with the brambles and nettles, so we had met. We now found he did not believe in letter-boxes, taking the view that it was his duty to deliver any post he had directly into the hands of the addressee. As our front door took the full force of the wind blowing up the glen, he had, of course, to stand in out of the elements as he rummaged in his bag, and this led to an invitation into the kitchen for a cup of tea.

The cup of tea rarely lasted less than a full hour, and we soon knew a lot more about Sean and about Glencullen. To our surprise, he knew the North; he had, in his younger days, been a cross-country runner, and to my amazement had actually competed against the legendary – to Northerners – Steve McCooke of East Antrim Harriers. He was also a doggy man, a breeder, and had been to many shows in Belfast.

He was full of surprises; he had been present at the Battle of Agincourt, though whether as a spectator or participant we were never too sure. Anyway, he had been there, when Henry V, in the person of Laurence Olivier, in 1944 not 1415, had led his troops in their famous charge across the slopes of the Powerscourt demesne for the cameras.

He had strong competition in the tea-drinking marathon stakes from the Human JCB, Johnny Cotter. We had moved into Glencullen before the outside work was completed, and Johnny was still laying paths and doing other tasks around the site. He had a lifetime of stories to tell, drawn from his service as a McAlpine fusilier on the roads of England, where he had taken his master's degree in the long-handled shovel, and also, probably, in tea-drinking.

Johnny had known the late Lil Doyle, and he recounted at length how, in the early days of our work on 'Whin Cottage', he had come down late to finish some job as night was falling. In the twilight he had rounded the porch and there was Lil, arms outstretched towards him, standing under the tree. He had let out a shriek, and was about to flee when he realised that it was not Lil – one of McD's workmen had left a rake sticking out of a barrel and draped an old coat jacket over it.

We found out from Johnny one reason why we had been able to buy the cottage without competition; Jack Flanagan, it seems, had fallen out with John Fox, and for a year or two had not been drinking there, preferring to walk the three miles to Enniskerry. John Fox was, as well as publican, also an auctioneer, valuer and estate agent for Glencullen, but there was no way Jack Flanagan was putting any business his way – so the cottage never went on the public market, and we were able to do our private deal.

We soon met John Fox too, not because we were great customers, or pub people at all, but because the only public phone in Glencullen was the one in the corridor between the bar and what was then called the new lounge – a small room with a fire place and easy chairs. Despite being on the waiting list for six months when we moved in, there was no word of a phone for us, which, given that I was a journalist, and that we had two children under the age of five, was a bit inconvenient.

Our car was another vehicle for meeting people. I had changed the Triumph Herald – its horn had somehow developed an intimate relationship with the steering wheel, which meant that it repeatedly gave loud and totally unpredictable blasts as you drove along, incurring the wrath of other drivers. So I bought a second hand Fiat 124, diplomatically doing business with the nearest garage, Mrs Graham's at Kilternan. We soon learned that it was a crime against humanity, if not a mortal sin, not to give a lift to anyone tramping the roads up to or down from Glencullen. People did not actually hitch, that was unnecessary as it could be assumed that no one was walking up or down for exercise or pleasure. The most they would do would be to glance expectantly over a shoulder. Having accepted a lift, it was only polite to engage in conversation with the benefactor, and that way our knowledge and our circle of acquaintance were rapidly broadened.

The car was an ice-breaker in other ways. We had no garage, and the car had to stand on the rough driveway running down from the road to our front door. When it rained in Glencullen it did so more horizontally than vertically.

Sugar Loaf from 'Whin Cottage'.

One thing we did not know about Fiats when we changed cars was their Italian dislike of damp, but we soon found out. This meant the only way to get ours to start in the morning was to free-wheel down the hill towards Wicklow, engaging the gears at a speed sufficient to startle the engine into life.

Fortunately, we lived at the top of a long and very steep hill. Unfortunately, the car was parked on our driveway, which meant it had to be pushed up a short distance of rough unsurfaced pathway onto the road, before it could be launched in the direction of the Devil's Elbow at the foot of the hill. This was a Herculean task, and that was how we met Mary Parker. One morning, with Katherine at the wheel, I was straining my biceps trying to budge the Fiat when a dark-haired young lady, who was striding up the road, called out to ask if I needed a hand.

Gallantly I said I thought it would be too much for her, but she laughed and put her shoulder to the back bumper with immediate results. She soon joined the long-distance tea-drinkers in our kitchen, and remained a friend for our whole time in Glencullen, and afterwards. She lived with her uncle and her four children, two or three fields below us, so was a daily passer up the hill behind our house.

The day came when the downhill charge proved insufficient for a saturated Fiat, and I found myself stranded at Glencullen bridge, straddling the border between Dublin and Wicklow, and going nowhere. The first time this happened, Tom Kennedy blithely shunted me into life, driving his own powerful vehicle up to my rear bumper and shoving. After a mile or so of an intermittent game of dodgems, the Fiat gave in and coughed into life.

The next time it happened, on a wet dark night, there was no Tom Kennedy around, and I had to seek help elsewhere. Christy Mahon, I was told, was my only man. I thought I had wandered into a J. M. Synge drama as I hiked up to Fox's to phone the number I had been given. Christy turned out to be a genius of a mechanic, who lived half way down the road to Kilternan, and who seemed to find nothing unusual or unreasonable in being asked to leave his fireside and rescue someone he had never met, stranded in the middle of nowhere. It was his first of several Good Samaritan impersonations.

It was through Mary Parker that we eventually mastered the wilderness that was the lower half of our new garden. Into the jungle of brambles and nettles our builder had dumped an abundance of rubble, old fence posts and wire, timber, tree roots and assorted debris. In the first spring we were there, the brambles and nettles had taken this to their bosom and knitted it into an impenetrable tumulus. Noting my feeble efforts to tackle it, my neighbours told me I needed a plough in to shift it.

Where would I find a plough? Mary Parker said she was sure her Uncle Peter, with whom she lived, would do it for us. She said she would ask him. We heard no more until one morning Peter, with another farmer, John Davis, arrived with tractor and plough and within a few hours had cleared the whole area and ploughed it, leaving neat piles of rescued granite to one side. I asked them what I owed them, and they flatly refused to take any payment. It was work for a neighbour. With difficulty I persuaded them to take a fiver to cover a drink or two in Fox's.

So our entry into the social life of Glencullen was incidental or even accidental. One reason it happened in that way was that, not being Catholic, we were not at mass, nor were our children going to the school. Glencullen generally did not cater for non-Catholics. We had enrolled our eldest child, who was just reaching school-age, in the nearest Protestant national school at Kilternan, three miles down the mountain, and were getting to know other parents there, but none of them lived in Glencullen.

Shortly after we moved in, I was hacking away at brambles in the bottom of the site when a loud voice hailed me in a strong country accent from the gateway at the top. 'How's the man?' it enquired in the ringing tones of authoritative bonhomie, and a formidable looking cleric advanced towards me with his hand out-stretched. I put down my shovel and took the hand, declaring myself to be Dennis Kennedy.

'Welcome', he said, and getting straight down to business, 'We'll be seeing you at Mass, I hope.'

'Not likely' I said, smiling 'I'm not a Catholic.'

He was visibly taken aback. 'Are you not, now?' he remarked, and seemed very nonplussed. After the exchange of a few pleasantries, he bade me good-bye, and we never saw him again. I think it had never entered his mind that anyone moving into Glencullen might not be a Catholic, and he had no idea how to react.

A few months later, in the late spring of that first year, I was using a crude sprinkler on a new bit of lawn I had managed to plant in an area rescued from the rubble and the brambles, when a passing neighbour accosted me from the gate.

'Hey,' he said amiably, 'You're not supposed to be doing that.'

'Doing what?'

'Watering the garden. Did you not know there's a ban on it? The reservoir above is very low after this dry spell, and some people have no pressure at all.'(Glencullen had only fairly recently, as the result of a self-help scheme, acquired its own public water supply, fed from a small tank-reservoir buried in the top of a hill above the village.)

'No one told me, and the pressure here is great.'

'Wasn't it announced at Mass last Sunday, and anyway you are about the lowest house in the scheme so you have no worry about pressure?'

'If it was announced at Mass it must apply to Catholics only. So I am OK.' I replied with a smile. 'Fair enough,' he laughed 'You could be right, but I would go easy on it just the same.'

And so I did. But much later, in the years to come, I often thought back on that exchange as emblematic of life as a Protestant in the wholly Catholic Republic. I had had nothing but a kind welcome in Glencullen, no one had remarked on religion, and in no way had I been discriminated against – but the life of the glen was Catholic, and it was assumed that anyone living in it was Catholic. All announcements about village matters, whether to do with the water, or the noise from the quarry, or the calling of a public meeting or anything else, were made at Mass. That was sufficient.

Not even our close neighbours, with whom we had become friendly, had thought of telling us about the water problem. It had been announced at Mass, and was therefore public knowledge. Glencullen, like the Republic itself, had no objection to Protestants living in it, but never thought of modifying its Catholic ways to accommodate them. That idea just never occurred. It was left to Protestants to make their own accommodation.

Four

Why Dublin?

What was I doing in Dublin anyway? Born and brought up in Lisburn in County Antrim, I was an enthusiastically evangelical Protestant. All my relations, on both my father's and mother's sides, were also evangelical Protestants, or, in one or two rare cases, had backslid from being such. All my family connections were in Lisburn, Ballymena, Portadown or Lurgan, and I had just returned from several years as a Lutheran missionary in Ethiopia. (To be exact, I had been a journalist employed by a Lutheran World Federation radio station, but, as His Imperial Majesty Haile Selassie, in his infinite wisdom, had decreed that missionaries should be exempt from income tax, we were all classified as missionaries.)

True, my wife Katherine, whom I had married three years earlier in Belfast, was from Dublin and her family was as Catholic as mine was Protestant, but we had been married in a Presbyterian church and had started married life among the Lutherans. Besides, it had very much been my decision to come back to Dublin, not Belfast, to Ireland, not Britain or anywhere else.

The South, or the Free State as we Northerners still called it, had held a romantic fascination for me since I had first encountered it on a childhood trip across Carlingford Lough from Warrenpoint to Omeath, and then on a post-war holiday in Dublin, feasting on ice-cream and ration-free sweets. After that there were occasional forays to Dundalk in an uncle's Morris, and one or two heroic trips by train to support Lisnagarvey in the Irish Senior Cup Final at Londonbridge Road.

There is a persistent myth that Protestants in Northern Ireland are taught no Irish history at school. Not true: even in Loyalist Lisburn we learned all about 1641, 1798, and 1848. (1916 was too recent – history stopped at the start of the Great War.) We were on familiar terms with Owen Roe O'Neill, Rinuccini and the Confederation of Kilkenny, Wolfe Tone, Daniel O'Connell and Charles Stewart Parnell. By the time I arrived at Queen's University to study history I had contracted a mild Nationalist virus. At Queen's, large doses of Irish history, frequent trips to student conferences in Dublin, Cork and Galway, hockey matches in Dublin for Queen's against UCD and Trinity, and excursions to climb Lugnaquillia, Carrauntoohil, Errigal, Brandon and Croagh Patrick, all ensured that my exposure to things southern increased during my student days.

I was sufficiently transfixed by all things Irish at Queen's to enrol in beginners' Irish language classes offered by the Gaelic Society, and who knows where they might have led had they not clashed, after a couple of weeks, with a Study Group organised by the Bible Union. (Certain things were sacrosanct.)

It was while a student that I became enamoured of another thing Irish – *The Irish Times.* I read it, free, in the university library almost daily, and delighted in Myles na gCopaleen's Cruiskeen Lawn, the witty 'pup' leaders, and, particularly, the Northern Letter. In those days, the mid-1950s, the North was, like London, still sufficiently remote from Dublin to merit a weekly despatch rather than large daily doses of news or comment. What I liked about The Northern Letter was that it dealt with serious issues in a way that was funny and irreverent. (Cecil Deeney, later to be a friend and colleague on the *Belfast Telegraph,* was the author of most of them.)

A year after graduating, and more or less by accident, I became a journalist myself. Early in 1959 I had been short-listed for a job with the National Trust, and called for interview. On the interviewing panel was John E. Sayers, Joint Managing Editor of the *Belfast Telegraph.* The interview went very well, and I sensed that I had impressed Mr Sayers. A week or so later I was told, very unofficially by another member of the panel, that I was likely to get the post. I waited, confident that my future was settled. Then came the public announcement that the post had been filled, and not by me. It was a great let-down; I had no idea what I was going to do. After graduating I had tried

part-time teaching for several months – long enough to learn that I was never
going to be a teacher – and now I was jobless and without prospects.

At a loss to know where to look for work, never mind a career, I thought
of writing to Mr Sayers and asking him for a job. So I did; I reminded him
of the National Trust interview, and said how disappointed I had been. The
only evidence of journalistic ability that I could produce was one article,
published in *Gown*, Queen's University's student newspaper, in my final year.
That was a one-off, which I had been asked to write. I had played no part in
student journalism, or even in student politics, though, if I had remembered,
I could have claimed to have been published in both the *Belfast Telegraph*

Rewarding view from top of Slemish.

and *The Irish Press.*

In my student days I had been secretary of the Queen's Photographic Society when Jack Sayers had written to the Society encouraging undergraduates to submit photos to him for publication in the *Telegraph.* I sent him one I had taken from the top of Slemish, showing St Patrick's wishing chair and the patchwork of Antrim fields below. It appeared on St Patrick's Day 1956, and I received two guineas. Almost a year later I had a letter from someone called Douglas Gageby in *The Irish Press,* asking if he could have the same picture for the *Press* for that St Patrick's Day. It duly appeared and I received three guineas. I little guessed that I would spend almost twenty years of my working life with one or other of those two remarkable men as my editor.

Jack Sayers had almost certainly forgotten the photo, but he liked the article, perhaps because it had attacked Brian Faulkner for his stance in a row over admitting Catholics to membership of the Unionist Party, and at that period Faulkner was the *bête noire* of the liberal *Telegraph.* Sayers called me in for an interview, and offered me a job as a reporter; 'bottom of the list' he said, and I would be required to master typing (forty words a minute) and shorthand (one hundred words a minute) within six months. It was an experiment, he said, the paper had never before employed a graduate as a reporter, but he had discussed the idea with Sir Eric Ashby, the then Vice-Chancellor of Queen's, and they had both agreed that it was an idea worth trying.

So at the end of August 1959, I became a reporter on *the Belfast Telegraph,* with a starting salary of £11 9s 0d a week. I could now afford to buy my own copy of *The Irish Times.* I did so every morning, with much pleasure, from the veteran news-seller with a stall on Royal Avenue. After several days he remarked, as he handed me the folded copy;

'Why on earth are you buying that?'

'Why not? What's wrong with it?' I replied, expecting a tirade against the Free State and all its works.

'Nothing at all, but it's the dearest paper on the stand.'

I smiled and walked on. As a thrifty Northerner he was just worried that a fresh-faced young fellow should be so reckless with his cash.

Working as a journalist in the *Telegraph* in those days did not mean many markings south of the Border. In five years I can recall only three such excursions – one to cover a Methodist annual conference in Cork, (the Sayers, who ran the *Telegraph,* were Methodists). Another was to do a series of interviews with civil servants in Dublin on how the Lemass-O'Neill meetings had impacted on their work. Not overmuch, it seemed; one senior official walked over to a filing cabinet, lifted out a thick file and said, 'It's like this – for every file we have, we have opened a new folder, and we label it The North'. Then I had an entirely unusual brief from Jack Sayers to go for a week wherever I liked in the South and talk to people about the North and their perceptions of it. That took me to Athlone, Thurles, Limerick, Bandon, Cork and Carlow. At Bandon I stumbled upon a by-election count, and had my first introduction to the mysteries of PR and the single transferable vote.

However, my munificent salary enabled me to buy a Vespa scooter, which, in my own time, transported me and my then girlfriend to the furthest quarters of the South, including exotic locations like Valentia Island, Achill and Glenmalure. After a series of tumbles from the scooter, a second-hand Ford increased the scope for adventure. I also began exploring the more remote fringes of Southern journalism. Substituting for a friend, I had a couple of articles published in *Hibernia*. I even applied for a job with Bord Fáilte, which had advertised for a rep in Belfast. I was called for interview in Dublin, but did not get the job. Nor did they ever refund my train fare.

But my journalism must have been improving, for, in 1963, it won me a fellowship from an American foundation which gave me a full year in the United States, plus the opportunity to travel around the world on my way home. I had applied for it in early 1963, but had not been told I had won it until early August, and given one week to make it to New York. Sayers was on holiday, so I could not ask him for leave of absence. Instead I left him a note saying I was going, and might or might not be back in a year's time. He was more than a bit miffed, and wrote me a sharp note saying there might, or might not, be a job for me in a year's time.

But he relented, and in mid-1964 wrote to me offering me the post of chief leader-writer if I returned. So I did, and began, in October 1964, to enjoy my new pontifical role, but at the same time growing ever more discontented with life in the North. All that was before, in 1965, I married Katherine, a colleague on the paper, a Dubliner who had joined it during my absence in America. Suddenly I had a family connection with the South, a new circle of Dublin friends, and a base for regular week-end visits. Even so I never thought of going to live there.

My short journalistic career to that point had seen the end of the Brookeborough era and the advent of Terence O'Neill, a transition warmly welcomed by the *Telegraph* and particularly by my editor, Jack Sayers. I never shared his enthusiasm for O'Neill, whose patrician liberalism seemed to me rather vague, consisting more of good intentions than actual reform. A few years after I joined the 'Telly' – as the *Telegraph* is always referred to in Belfast, there was renewed interest in the disadvantages suffered by Catholics in Northern Ireland, particularly in the areas of public housing and employment. Against the background of the swelling civil rights movement in America, some British politicians and newspapers began to ask questions about discrimination in Ulster.

In 1964 BBC Television, in one of its news magazine programmes, looked in particular at the situation in Fermanagh, and the resulting programmes caused a stir in the province, partly because of the newness of TV, and its vast impact, and partly because the programmes were highly critical of Unionist politicians, above all in the allocation of local government houses.

As a result, Jack Sayers sent me down to Fermanagh and Tyrone to do a series of articles, published in November 1964 under the title *Religious Houses,* which did me no favours with the Unionist establishment, but gained me public approbation from one member of the Catholic hierarchy. I found myself having increasing freedom to criticise Unionism over issues such as the name chosen for the new city to link Portadown and Lurgan (Craigavon), over the name originally voted by Unionists for the new Lagan bridge in Belfast (Carson – though in the end it became The Queen Elizabeth Bridge) and over the decision to locate the new university not in Derry, but in Coleraine.

By the mid-1960s the journalists of the *Belfast Telegraph* had been dubbed 'the Snivelling Scribblers of Royal Avenue'. The sobriquet was bestowed upon us by the Reverend Ian R.K. Paisley, then a rapidly-rising Unionist firebrand, scourge of liberals, enemy of ecumenism and rooter-out in chief of Red Socks (i.e. Papal) influence. The *Telegraph* under Jack Sayers qualified for regular denunciation by Paisley under a variety of heads. As his chief leader-writer from 1964 to 1966, I was, I suppose, a chief sniveller.

Our leaders were not signed, and while they appeared on the front page every day it was assumed almost no one read them. But they had at least one faithful follower, who scrutinised their every word – the Revd Paisley. He frequently found a text from within them to analyse and condemn in his Sunday sermons, but it still came as a bit of a shock when one of my own phrases was not just dammed from the pulpit, but became the occasion of a protest march on the offices of the *Telegraph*. I had suggested in a leader that

Paisley and his followers represented 'the lunatic fringes of Unionism'.

There was something extremely flattering to a young leader-writer in having such notice taken of his words. So much so that I could not resist the temptation to turn up at the appointed time and place for the protest – the front of Belfast City Hall on a cold November Saturday night – and follow the march, heavily cloaked in anonymity and a tweed coat.

Donegall Place and Royal Avenue were almost deserted. The small column of a hundred or so shuffled off, led by the Reverend brandishing his Bible. We were an odd mixture of respectable middle-aged couples, many carrying Bibles, some pious young people, and an assortment of sturdy youths sporting Linfield scarves and expressing themselves in language that suggested they were not regulars at the Free Presbyterian services. Plus, shuffling alongside, one very anonymous leader-writer.

As well as his Bible, Paisley was clutching a large piece of paper which, he had announced, he would nail to the front door of the *Belfast Telegraph*, thereby expressing his convictions in the manner in which Martin Luther had expressed his at the church in Wittenberg some time earlier. (He had, he said, brought hammer and nails with him for the purpose.)

What I knew, and the Reverend obviously did not, was that the Thomson organisation which now owned the *Telegraph*, had, in its brashness and affluence, recently refurbished the front entrance of the *Telegraph* office, then at the corner on Royal Avenue, replacing the old wooden door with a new all-glass door set in an all-glass surround.

When the march reached the *Telegraph*, Paisley mounted the steps, addressed the crowd, read his Theses (there were not, fortunately, ninety-five of them), produced his hammer and turned to the door. What treachery was this, he demanded. The Thomson organisation, he roared, had deliberately put in a glass front to stop Reformation Protestants making their point in the forceful Lutheran way. What duplicity! What else would you expect from the Snivelling Scribblers of Royal Avenue?

But he was not going to be defeated. Someone, surely, had a roll of sticky tape with them? You, Sergeant, how about you, he flatteringly appealed to the RUC constable on duty. Someone (I hope not the RUC man) did indeed produce some tape, and the protest was stuck to the glass panel. Not the same as hammering it firmly home with a large nail, but not a bad tribute to the anonymous words of a young Snivelling Scribbler.

At Easter 1965 my wife-to-be took me away from all this on a voyage of discovery to Inisheer, the smallest of the Aran Islands. Katherine had stayed there before, and was anxious to show me somewhere really different. So we drove to Galway, stayed overnight and took the *Naomh Eanna* the next morning. It was a blustery day in early April, and Katherine spent most of the three-hour trip prostrate on a seat, moaning and groaning. Then it was out an opening in the side of the boat near the water line, and a jump down into the waiting arms of the boatmen in the currach below, for an even bumpier ride back to the beach and a splash through the surf. Inisheer had no harbour, nor any jetty big enough to allow the ferry from Galway to dock, so all goods and people had to transfer into currachs well out at sea.

We had made no arrangements, but headed up the beach to the cottage where Katherine had stayed before. We got a great welcome from Andy, but his sister, the woman of the house, was over in Galway for a week, so there was no question of us finding a berth there for three nights. As most of the negotiations were in Irish, I was not too sure whether the problem was allowing two unmarried young people to stay inadequately chaperoned, with the woman of the house away, or simply that there would be no one to feed us.

So we set off around the cottages, with Katherine politely inquiring if there was any question of 'beirt seomra'[i] for three nights. We had little success until we arrived up at the Weaver's, which Andy had suggested as a last port of call. He had told us the weaver was married to the Inish Mean woman – she was from the neighbouring island – 'a fine block of a woman' he assured us, and as they had no children they might have room. They had, and we were allocated two attics under the eaves.

The Weaver and his fine block of a wife were excellent hosts. We shared the cottage with their handsome dog, and from time to time, a flock of chickens who kept slipping in at the open door. When they did, the Weaver would roar at the dog 'Cuir amach an chearc'[ii], and the dog, a native speaker, would rout the invaders. The dog's party piece was to chase his own tail furiously at the command 'Teampaill'[iii] from the Weaver.

That first afternoon, after we had left our bags with The Weaver, we wandered back to the strand in time to see the last of a number of cattle being loaded onto the *Naomh Eanna*. With a rope attached to its head, each beast

---

(i) Two rooms.

(ii) Put out the hen.

(iii) Turn.

was driven into the surf, and then obliged to swim behind a currach out to the boat, where it was hoisted by crane in a cradle onto the deck.

We watched the drama until the end, and stayed on the beach until the *Naomh Eanna* disappeared over the horizon. I still remember having the distinct impression that we were on board a ship, and that we had steamed away from the mainland, represented by the *Naomh Eanna*. This feeling of being adrift on a world apart was reinforced the next morning when we awoke to find the island shrouded in mist. It soon lifted and we had three brisk but sunny days to explore the island, to visit the ruins of St Kevin's church, then half buried in the dunes that threatened to engulf the houses closest to the strand, to trek over to the other side of the island to see the shipwreck, the small coaster beached, years earlier, high and dry on the rocky shore, and to climb up to the small ruined castle on the highest point of the island.

Everyone we met was courtesy itself, including Orla the Dane, a latter-day Viking who had turned up on Inisheer years earlier, and had stayed, setting up a one man-craft industry – I still have the coloured woven 'crios' I bought from him that day. The island was entirely Irish-speaking, and older people apologised to us for their poor English, but were happy to talk away to the strangers. We were the only visitors; tourists would come in the summer, and there would be the annual invasion of schoolchildren coming to learn Irish, but for the moment, in early April, we had Inisheer and the people of Inisheer to ourselves. I had read *The Islandman*, by Tomás O'Crohan, and Maurice O'Sullivan's *Twenty Years a' Growing*, so was already smitten by the romance of island life, even if those books told of the Blaskets, not the Aran Islands. But Inisheer on that first trip was not a romantic invention – it was a wonderful, romantic, reality.

The islandmen still wore jerseys and rough tweed trousers, tied round the middle with a 'crios', and the women still dressed in bright-red woollen petticoats and shawls. Their concerns were not what was happening in Dublin or Belfast, but whether 'the schame' – the experimental planting of special grasses in the dunes in an attempt to stop the relentless march inland of the fine beach sand – would work, and which of the island's two pubs served the better pint.

My already romanticised view of rural Ireland was much enhanced, and we vowed to return to Inisheer.

Thanks to my new links to Dublin I found I had a direct line to Irish history. On my now frequent visits to Sandymount in Dublin, I met an elderly family friend of Katherine and her mother. Now partially bed-ridden, she was delighted to have someone to talk to, and she took to me, probably because I was ready to listen, and eager to hear her many stories, but also, she insisted, because I was a 'Northern', and the 'Northerns' were decent people, as were the British and the Germans, but not the French – they were dirty.

Just where and when she had formed these strong views I have no idea. She had been a widow since the 1920s, her doctor husband having died after the Great War, and she had retreated into privacy thereafter. But just how much a living link she was to a distant past I discovered one day chatting to her about her girlhood in late Victorian Dublin. Recounting how she often went out to tea on Sunday afternoons with two sisters called Parnell, she told me all about them, where they lived, what they looked like, adding finally, as an afterthought; 'Their brother was that politician fellow'.

She was herself a veteran of 1916. She loved to tell the story of how she had been sent, on the Wednesday or Thursday of Easter week, to walk towards the city in search of bread, as none was to be had in her suburb. At one of the bridges over the Grand Canal she was stopped by a British Tommy. She asked him was it all over. 'Yes ma'am', I 'ope so', he replied, 'Now we're just waiting for the 'ill tribes'.

By that time, 1966, I had had enough of Northern Ireland. I had inherited the role of 'stringer' in Belfast for the *Sunday Times* from my Telly colleague Cal McCrystal, and now there was a tentative offer of a job in London on their new Insight Team. There was also a possibility of a post with the Lutheran World Federation at their radio station in Addis Ababa. This latter, though not well paid, included a furnished bungalow and a totally new horizon which did not include Northern Ireland.

I was, by then, sufficiently disenchanted with Britishness to have swapped my blue passport for a green one, and sufficiently uninterested in whether Wilson or Heath reigned supreme in Downing Street that I plumped for Addis Ababa. London I could go to any time, a job in Addis Ababa was a once in a lifetime chance. So I persuaded my wife, then about five months pregnant, that a bungalow in Addis was infinitely preferable to a mortgage in Belfast, or London.

For the next two years plus, my knowledge of things Irish, North or South, depended on the BBC World Service, a once a week copy of *The Irish Times* which arrived haphazardly by airmail, and the monthly *Bulletin* of the Department of External Affairs in Dublin. When the first copy of the *Bulletin* arrived it was addressed to me at PO Box 654 Addis Ababa, Utopia. Thereafter, for my entire stay, two copies arrived each month, one correctly addressed, the other, with unfailing optimism, directed to 'Utopia'.

We also had one direct contact with External Affairs. By 1968 the situation in Ethiopia had become lively, with student riots, criticism of the Emperor, and weekly rumours of a *coup d'état*. The American Embassy had organised its nationals into emergency groups, with arrangements for the alerting, assembling and evacuation of US citizens, complete with practice runs. The British did not go that far, but did put some arrangements in place. At my wife's pleading, I wrote to the Department in Dublin to ask what measures they were recommending for Irish citizens in this worrying situation, and what arrangements did they have with other embassies to look after us. A couple of weeks later I received a letter advising me that in the event of any trouble in Ethiopia, I should write to the Department of External Affairs, Iveagh House, Dublin 2.

Reassured that Iveagh House was keeping a cool head as regards Ethiopia, we soldiered on. But the end of my contract was looming in the near distance, and we had to make up our minds if we would renew it. We decided not to renew, partly because of some health problems, but more because of a developing allergy to missionaries and all their works. I was also becoming impatient to return to Ireland; things were happening, both North and South.

Just what would happen in the North I did not know, but the growing agitation over discrimination had been joined on the political scene by the rising tide of Nationalism prompted by the 1966 anniversary of 1916, and 'civil rights' were now high on everyone's agenda. In the South, employment was up as new factories came in and emigration was down. Vatican Two had loosened up the Catholic monolith, Donogh O'Malley had decreed free secondary education, Trinity was to be merged with UCD, Noel Browne was back. And the seventies were going to be Socialist.

In Addis Ababa another link with *The Irish Times* had manifested itself in the shape of Edgar Brennan, who had joined our newsroom from the BBC. A TCD man, Church of Ireland to the core, with an encyclopaedic knowledge of Dublin tram and bus routes, he had begun his journalistic career as a sub on *The Irish Times*, sharing a table with luminaries such as Steptoe senior, who as Wilfred Brambell, was then earning a journalistic crust.

I should certainly go and work for *The Irish Times*, was Edgar's advice.

There was some fellow called Gageby running it now, but never mind him, I should go and see Matt Chambers, a decent man, who would sort something out for me.

So in the summer of 1968, as the world was mourning Bobby Kennedy, Dubcek was getting worried in Prague, the Civic Group was deploring the destruction of Georgian Dublin, and as RTE was advertising for a Senior Radio Executive at a salary of not less than £2,600, we returned to Ireland, to Dublin, not Belfast.

In Ethiopia I had continued my Irish studies with the help of Risteard O' Glaisne's *Bun-Ghaelige* (complete with tape). The first phrase I learned was 'Cuir an buideal ar an bhord'[(i)]; I was soon to appreciate how central to the culture of Dublin journalists that instruction was.

(i) Put the bottle on the table.

Five

Badly out of Touch

I arrived in Dublin high on a mixture of optimism, naivety, and a sense of adventure, all overlaid by a pleasant romantic Nationalism. Going to Addis had been an adventure, but then I had been going to a pre-arranged job, not to mention a bungalow. Now I was leaping into the real unknown, with no job, nowhere to live, and two infants under the age of three.

My first port of call was that decent man, Matt Chambers. He had been Chief Sub in *The Irish Times*, and was now in a more elevated position exercising overall supervision of the production of the paper from a solitary desk behind the Chief Sub. He was charming, and arranged for me to meet Douglas Gageby, who, with bustling good humour, told me he would love to give me a job, but the only thing he could offer was a bottom of the list reporter, and, he insisted, I was far too well qualified for that. RTE would jump at me, he said, and there were other possibilities. I would be mad to settle for the lowly post he could offer. Anyway, he added as I left, if I was still looking for a job in a couple of months, I could always come back and see him.

So I did the rounds. I was interviewed by RTE for a job in radio. Jack White, Jim Maginnis and Des Fisher were on the panel. I outlined my experience in America and Africa as well as Northern Ireland, listing the people I had interviewed, from Bobby Kennedy to Julius Nyrere, via Jomo Kenyatta, Sadruddin Aga Khan, Hubert Humphrey, Lyndon Johnston, Senator Fulbright, Charles de Gaulle and John Betjeman. (I was laying it on a bit – some I had interviewed, others I had questioned in a press conference, and others I had been, in a journalistic capacity, in the same room as, and would have asked a question if I had had the chance.) Then one of the panel, I think it was Des, looked at me and asked:

'How long did you say you've been away?'

About two and half years, I told him.

'You must be very out of touch.'

That was that. A while later I phoned Douglas Gageby again. He took me to lunch in the Russell, with Donal Foley. He was as breezy as at the first meeting, gave me the job, apologising for its lowly status but saying who knew but I might be the editor in ten years time. That cheered me up greatly; I later realised he said that to everyone who joined the staff.

So I started in Westmoreland Street in August 1968. (The front office of the paper, and its famous clock, were both then still in Westmoreland Street, though the editorial entrance, aptly enough, was round the corner in Fleet Street.) I began as the lowest ranker on the reporters' list, dependent on the demands of the day and the whims of whoever was manning the news desk. First day in, Donal Foley was at a loss over what to do with me, so he asked me to write a colour piece on the bin men's strike, which had been on for some days. Take a look around and see what's happening on the streets, he told me. How long, I asked. Oh not too long, just about 800 words.

I replied that in my recent journalism that was a full length feature article, and I was not sure I still knew 800 words. He looked bewildered and mumbled something to the effect that I might give it a try anyway. He had no complaints when I handed it in later that day. There followed several visits to the Dublin Horse Show, with endless phoning in of results enlivened by high drama in the Aga Khan Cup when Tommy Brennan parted company with Tubbermac right in front of the press box, and the horse had to be put down.

The following week I was saved from routine by the Soviet invasion of Czechoslovakia, not by being sent to Prague, but having the job of following up all local angles and coordinating much of the coverage from abroad. As it turned out, a young Dubliner had found himself in Prague when it all happened, and the stories he began sending us helped launch Vincent Browne on his journalistic career.

Starting work as a reporter on *The Irish Times* a bare two months after arriving in Dublin from Africa meant a very sudden immersion into a new world. I may have deemed myself as Irish as the next man, but almost everything was totally new to me – the institutions, the politicians and public figures, even the geography of Dublin. I had a great deal to learn, but the learning was rapid, and I soon felt at home, comfortable.

Small things did surprise me, and served to remind me that I was living in a different society. A news item in those early days intrigued me; it was the annual Blessing of the Fleet at Dublin Airport by a Catholic Church dignitary. I knew that blessing the fleet was a traditional ceremony at coastal towns and villages all around the Mediterranean, but that was the local priest blessing the boats of his fishermen parishioners. This was a Bishop blessing the Boeings of the national airline. It seemed funny to me – both amusing and peculiar.

Then we acquired our first ever television, and I had the shock of the Angelus. I must have heard it on Radio Eireann as a child, but seeing the television screen frozen with a holy picture as the bell tolled at six in the evening and the country waited for the news, was very peculiar.

One of my first markings for *The Irish Times* was the opening of a small exhibition in Merrion Square. I wandered up to find that the ceremony was being performed by the Director of the Arts Council, a most urbane, and indeed polished gentleman, who turned out to be Father Donal O'Sullivan S.J. No doubt he was well fitted for the job, but to have a Jesuit priest as the salaried director of a semi-state body? Very odd.

Another surprise awaited me when I became Diplomatic Correspondent and learned that the Dean of the Diplomatic Corps in Dublin was the Papal Nuncio, and that the Nuncio was automatically the Dean of the Corps. My experience up to then, in countries where I had lived or travelled as a journalist, had been that the longest serving ambassador in post was Dean. In Catholic countries around the world, I was told, the Nuncio was always Dean. I could not help noting that the Nunciature was not in Ballsbridge, as most embassies were, but in that old seat of British Vice-regal power, the Phoenix Park, and indeed in Ashdown Lodge, once the home of the Under Secretary for Ireland. Was it symbolic that the Nuncio shared the privilege of living in the Park with the President and the Ambassador of the United States? All very odd.

But perhaps not odd at all in a country where the Church and the State worked in close partnership in the provision of education, health care and much else. But I was not particularly worried. After all, the seventies were going to be socialist, weren't they?

That first winter in *The Irish Times* was fairly bleak. I had been obliged to come down from the quarter deck reserved for the officer class of journalists, like Leader-Writers, or News Editors, and bend my back with the ratings. Odd job markings, stints at Night Town and similar graveyard shifts were less than fulfilling. Physically, the *Irish Times* office, with its scruffy news room and disintegrating typewriters, was a far cry from my airy, sun-bathed and very modern newsroom in Addis Ababa. The salary was modest, certainly not enough to offer any quick relief from my housing problems.

At a very low point in January or February 1969 I applied to a PR firm run by an old acquaintance from Belfast, and was offered a job in its new Dublin office. A bit horrified at myself for even applying, I immediately turned it down, deciding to stick it out in Westmoreland Street. I was, after all, learning to find my way around Dublin, and getting to know something of the substance and personalities of both press and politics.

I was also beginning to absorb some of the culture shock of moving to Dublin. One of my new colleagues invited me to a party – I think it was a house-warming – in a grand house in Waterloo Road. The invitation was for 8pm. Katherine could not go, so I drove there on my own, making sure that I arrived at ten past eight, knowing well that Southerners were some-what relaxed about time. I found the house, mounted the impressive flight of granite steps, and knocked at the door. There was no response, and after knocking more vigorously I saw the door was in fact open, so I pushed it and stepped inside.

All lights were on in a large hallway with a grand staircase leading up from it, but no one was to be seen. I gave some shouts of 'Anybody there?' and these eventually produced, to my intense embarrassment, a strange figure at the top of the staircase; she was wearing, I think, curlers or a shower cap, was wrapped in a dressing gown, and was not best pleased. She was my friend's wife, my friend had gone off to collect a barrel of porter, I was far too early, so would I mind going off to the pub for a drink or two. I scuttled away and did not return for an hour; even then, I was among the first arrivals. I never did fully adjust to Dublin time.

I was also becoming aware of the some of the pitfalls awaiting a new-comer not conversant with the traditions and culture of the *Irish Times*. I soon learned that there were three cardinal sins that anyone writing for the paper had to avoid, on pain of, if not dismissal, then the very public rage of Gageby. The first sin was to use the phrase 'the Irish army'. It was THE army, and there was only one where old-soldier Gageby was concerned. Second was to call Britain 'the mainland' – that was continental Europe, Britain was 'the other island'. And a third commandment was never to write about 'the Queen'; all queens had to be identified, whether Queen Victoria, Queen Salote or Queen Elizabeth II, they were all the same to us in the IT.

Wesley Boyd, our Diplomatic Correspondent, was lured away to RTE early in 1969, and to the surprise of many, including myself, I was appointed to the post in March. Lionel Flemming, who had retired as BBC Diplomatic Correspondent and returned to Dublin to rejoin his old paper, might have been the obvious replacement, but he had discovered a new obsession with the preservation of old Dublin and was writing vigorously in that area.

As Diplomatic Correspondent I was also a member of the paper's 'political staff'. In fact the title had been invented largely to lend dignity to Wesley Boyd's role as deputy political correspondent. By the time I was appointed, EEC membership was on the horizon, and Ireland was beginning to take a growing interest in development aid and in South Africa, and the United Nations. So, though I sometimes deputised for Michael McInerney, our veteran Political Correspondent, most of my involvement was with Ireland's external relations, not with domestic politics.

Apart, that is, from Northern Ireland. Such was the pace of events there in 1969, and the enormous demands placed on newspapers by them, that everyone, whatever distinguished title he went under in Westmoreland Street, found himself reporting from Belfast, or Derry, or Newry or Dungiven or Pomeroy. My first real bit of excitement had come in Newry, when I was covering a civil rights march and the ensuing minor riot in January 1969.

Peadar Carr, then of the *Cork Examiner*, and I were watching scuffles in the centre of the town late that evening when the RUC decided to clear the street, with truncheons drawn. We were, of course observers, and stayed to observe. Or at least we did until we realised that 'clearing the street' meant exactly that, at which point we took to our heels and raced for the safety of the Imperial Hotel in the square, narrowly ahead of the nearest truncheon. I got there just as the door was being slammed and made it in; Peadar was not so lucky, and caught a truncheon behind the ear. We pulled him bleeding into the lobby. He took it well, and regarded the wound as a badge of honour.

A month later I found myself nursing a minor injury. In the Stormont election of February 1969 I was in Castledawson to cover the contest in which Bernadette Devlin was challenging the squire of Castledawson, James Chichester-Clarke. On a freezing cold night I stood close to the handful of supporters gathered around Bernadette, on the main street. She was addressing a crowd that consisted mainly of jeering Paisleyites on the opposite pavement.

Having had enough of Bernadette's rhetoric, they launched a fusillade of missiles across the street, starting with potatoes but graduating to stones. I took a spud on the ear – a British Queen, I suppose, given its origin – and retired to file my story. I ended it with what I thought was a neat flourish, that 'the Paisleyites were leaving no stone unthrown in their opposition to Miss Devlin.'

When I read in the next day's paper that they were leaving no stone 'unturned' I called down all manner of retribution on the sub who had changed it. Back in Dublin I was approached by a smiling, affable sub-editor who was seeking me out to tell me he had caught a mistake in my copy the other night and had corrected it.

Later that year I was sent to cover the annual Apprentice Boys' parade in Derry on Tuesday 12 August. I arrived on Monday, and moved into a room in the City Hotel; I left the following Saturday and can't have spent more than a dozen hours in that bedroom. Monday night saw a modest overture to the violence that was to engulf Derry for the next four days, but it was enough to keep me phoning Dublin until 4a.m. with accounts of stone-throwing and petrol bombs in Bishop Street.

Tuesday was quiet enough until the afternoon, when the Apprentice Boys parade started passing through Waterloo Place on its way home. I was standing up the hill on Waterloo Street, just above the Place, yards away from the parade. About 3p.m. some of the youths from the Bogside, who had been jeering the marchers, started throwing stones at the parade. One enterprising young man produced a catapult and a supply of steel ball bearings which he proceeded to ping at the marchers.

The stones became larger, and some of those following the parade started throwing them back up the hill. One small lump of granite, about half the size of a tennis ball, landed near me; a boy, not more than ten or eleven years old, dashed to grab it and send it back, but I put my foot on it and told him it was mine. I put it in my coat pocket. It was still there when I made it back to the City Hotel at about 8a.m. the next morning, after a night of rioting, burning, police charges, barricades and desperate searches for any public phone that still worked, or any private phone on offer. I wondered what any policeman might have made of the stone in my pocket had I been stopped and searched. It rested on the mantelpiece in Whin Cottage for years, before it disappeared in an annual spring cleaning.

At the end of that hectic week, Douglas Gageby contacted me in Derry and asked me to meet him for dinner on Sunday night in the Dunadry Inn, then the most up-market hotel in the North. I drove to Dunadry, booked into sheer luxury, and had a long soak to wash away the dirt and dust of Derry. At dinner, Gageby told me he wanted me to get to New York as quickly as possible, to cover the Security Council's consideration of Ireland's attempt to raise the crisis at the UN.

Back in Monkstown on Monday, I was off again on Wednesday morning, dashing straight from the airport in New York to the UN building, just in time to get a seat in the Press Gallery at the Security Council to hear the beginning of the debate on Ireland's request, and to see Dr Paddy Hillery slipping into a seat at the end of the horseshoe table. I sat there in a daze listening to the delegate from the Soviet Union, from Ghana, to Paddy Hillery and to Lord Caradon all talking about Belfast and Derry, none of which any of them had ever visited, and even mentioning particular streets on which I had spent most of the previous week. As I wrote in *The Irish Times,* I wondered was it me or the world which had gone mad, or was it just Northern Ireland.

Anyway, the peculiar combination of the Bogside and the UN Security Council had got my career as Diplomatic Correspondent off to a flying start. It had also given me the chance to write analytical articles on the Northern Ireland problem, which I proceeded to do with enough regularity to try the patience of my editor. Those articles also, surprisingly perhaps, triggered a close and long-lasting friendship with Paddy Hillery, and later, with Jack Lynch, both of whom confessed privately, with disarming frankness, that up to that summer they had known nothing about the North.

Later in 1969, I had a phone call from External Affairs. An official said the Minister would like to talk to me, and could I come up to Iveagh House that afternoon, if I was free. I had met Hillery only briefly at the UN, and did not know him, so I said yes rather nervously, rather fearing a Ministerial reprimand for something I had written. I was shown into his splendid office in Iveagh House at 4p.m. – I had been there once before, briefly, after my appointment as Dip Cor earlier that year, to present my credentials, as it were, to the formidable Frank Aiken, who was still in office. I had been terribly impressed by the fact that Iveagh House was a turf-burning institution – in his office there was a roaring fire in the ornate grate, and a massive creel of turf beside it. I think it was still turf-fuelled when I met his replacement, Paddy Hillery, in the same room. Anyway there was a fire in the grate, and we sat talking, the two of us, for more than two hours.

He wanted to know all about the North, acknowledging frankly that he himself knew very little about it, and had never visited it. (In fact, he had been to Belfast on a day trip in March 1966 to speak, as Minister for Industry and Commerce, at a conference of Junior Chambers of Commerce from North and South.) He asked me lots of questions, and listened patiently to everything I had to say. By the time he led me to the front door of a deserted Iveagh House – everyone else had gone home – an odd friendship had begun to take root.

That autumn and winter I seemed to spend more time out of Dublin than in it. I was back at the UN in September for the General Assembly, and in mid-November I was despatched for four weeks to South Africa to write about apartheid on the eve of a controversial Springbok rugby tour of Britain and Ireland. The following year entry negotiations for the European Economic Community began, which meant almost monthly trips to Brussels and other EEC capitals.

I still found time to stumble into a brief but glorious sojourn as the Men's Fashion Correspondent of *The Irish Times*. Being drawn into a seminar in the Pearl Bar one evening I joined Donal Foley in some mild criticism of the Women's Page, then in the hands of Mary Maher and her new assistant, Maeve Binchy. Foley rather enjoyed provoking the wrath of Miss Maher, late of Chicago, and playing on the ample insecurities of Miss Binchy. His target that night was their coverage of fashion, and of men's fashion in particular. I rashly added my tuppence worth, to the effect that I could do it better myself, even if I knew nothing about men's fashion. I was immediately nominated for the job, and Foley took wicked pleasure in endorsing the appointment on the spot. Thus was born Campbell Kaye. I thoroughly enjoyed the six months that he lasted, and have the cuttings to prove it.

We had moved into 'Whin Cottage' in Glencullen in January 1971, and soon thereafter the Scandinavian countries and more distant locations such as Quebec and Japan were added to my travels. All this seriously interfered with finishing bits and pieces around the house, completing the decoration, expelling the mice that had come to regard Lil Doyle's place as their own, and creating a garden. It restricted the time available for exploring Glencullen, and getting to know all about it and its residents.

But it also made me appreciate still more its value as a wonderful retreat, as a place apart from riots and tear-gas, airports and planes, trains and buses, even traffic. At least that was for me; I think my wife, isolated for weeks on end with two young children, had a slightly different perspective.

Six

Glencullen

The Glencullen we began to explore was an odd sort of a place. It was not exactly a village, and the locals rarely used that word in reference to it. Glencullen meant the whole glen, and the population, then of around 500, was scattered along it, not just in the built-up stretch of road near the crossroads which included the 'new' church, the old ruined church, the graveyard, the school and the pub – and also, believe it or not, the Carnegie Library. But it had no real shop; when we moved in there were two 'sweetie' shops attached to houses along that stretch of road, selling little more than chocolate bars and ice-cream for children, and within a year or two both of them were closed. The nearest shops selling basic groceries were three miles away, in Stepaside, Enniskerry or Kilternan. I was very proud of living in a village that had no shops, but could boast a functioning public library.

Our Dublin friends had warned us about living so high up in the mountains, and about how cold it could get there. As we had recently been living in Addis Ababa at about 6,000 feet above sea level, Glencullen's 900 feet was no cause for concern. A close look at a large scale map showed me that the 800 foot contour line ran through my garden.

Glencullen's most celebrated building was Fox's Pub, since much marketed, promoted, extended and synthesized into almost a parody of an Irish country pub, but then known only to veterans of the *bona fide* days and to devotees of traditional music, for it had long been a venue for regular gatherings of fiddlers, tin whistlers and bodhrán drummers. Glencullen was remote enough to make Fox's a *bona fide* house for almost anyone who did not actually live in Glencullen, for it meant he could avail of the extended drinking hours legally allowed to genuine i.e. *bona fide*, travellers, defined as those who found themselves, out of hours, both in need of fortification and at least three miles from home. The *bona fide* rule survived until 1960.

Left: Glencullen from the road to Enniskerry, 'Whin Cottage' is centre left, nearest the camera.

Below: Fox's pub in the 1970s, before reinvention.

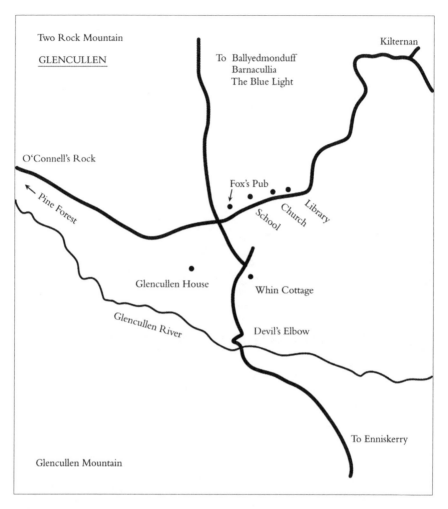

Map of Glencullen.

Convenient to Fox's was the parochial house, then an elegant Georgian-type dwelling, with granite steps up to its elevated front door. (It was subsequently demolished – tumbled as the locals would say – on the orders of the resident curate whose interests lay in things other than architecture.) Further along was the 'new' church, a small but very handsome granite structure, opened in 1909. The label 'new' was still applied to it because the shell of the old original church, built in 1830, had never been demolished, and stood along the road, a romantic ruin surrounded by trees and dressed overall in ivy.

Another handsome building, also made of granite, was the Carnegie Library, dating from 1907, not just a monument to the literacy of earlier generations of Glencullen residents, but a fully operational public library, doubling as a useful village hall. There were physical reminders too of earlier and different days in Glencullen in the shape of a dispensary and a police barracks, both having, long since, been converted into private dwellings.

But the glen's most distinguished building was Glencullen House, tucked away behind its 'grand gates' and avenue of beech trees less than half a mile from the pub. It was Glencullen's 'Big House', but a Big House with a difference or two. For a start it was not very big, not big at all. Even more unusual it was still in the hands of the Catholic family, the Fitz-Simons, who had first built it as a roadside farmhouse in the seventeenth century. At the end of the eighteenth century, or in the early nineteenth, it had been transformed by the addition of a new double-fronted Georgian section, complete with pillared portico, said to be the work of Francis Johnston, architect of the GPO in O'Connell Street, the Chapel Royal in Dublin Castle, St George's church in central Dublin, and overseer of the building of Nelson's Pillar. Glencullen owed its old church, school, police barracks, dispensary and library to the Fitz-Simon family's periodic largesse in the nineteenth century.

Our 'Whin Cottage', we later learned, had started life as a shepherd's cabin, built in 1829 by the Fitz-Simons at a cost of £30. That original building was now our shed, with the larger cottage added in about 1850, after the Famine when holdings were being consolidated.

The Christopher Fitz-Simon who had first built on the 'Whin Cottage' site in 1829 had been a close associate of Daniel O'Connell in the struggle, first for Catholic Emancipation, and then for Home Rule. Both he and his brother eventually sat at Westminster as O'Connellite MPs. At a dinner in Glencullen House on the 8 February 1823 O'Connell had formally proposed that they found a Catholic Association to revive the campaign for Emancipation.

The following year Christopher proposed marriage to O'Connell's eldest daughter, Ellen, as they sat on a rock below the house, and to this day the rock bears their engraved initials, and the date 1824. They were married in 1825 and Ellen became the chatelaine of Glencullen House, remaining so until her death in 1883, the last twenty-seven years of her life as a widow. In all she had twelve children, four of whom died as infants.

The portico of
Glencullen House,
added in the
early years of the
nineteenth century,
believed to be the
work of Francis
Johnston.

When we arrived in 1971 we knew nothing of Glencullen House, except
that it was occupied by 'the Colonel' and his wife, and had something to do
with Daniel O'Connell. Nor did we know anything at all about how the
hand of history had, from time to time, rested on Glencullen. My first indication that, while we had migrated to the back of beyond, we had not fallen
off the historical map of Ireland, came from an artist friend in Sandymount,
who could scarcely contain her excitement at the news that we had moved
into Glencullen, and was, frankly, shocked that I did not know that Red
Hugh O'Donnell and his companions had passed through the glen on their
famous escape from Dublin Castle at Christmas in 1591, or indeed that the
same Red Hugh had made it as far as the Three Rock Mountain on an
earlier escape, only to be recaptured in Glencullen.

We then heard about O'Connell's Rock at the top of the glen, almost as
far as the Pine Forest, and went up to have a look at it, and read the inscrip-
tion that told us Daniel O'Connell had addressed a mass meeting from it
on 23 July 1823. O'Connell was a frequent visitor to Glencullen House,
and used it as a quiet retreat near Dublin for private meetings with political
friends and contacts, and even, it is said, the odd Viceroy.

The Great Famine hit Glencullen in the mid-1840s, and Christopher
Fitz-Simon was appointed chairman of the Glencullen Relief Committee.
In June 1847 he was writing out to the 'large proprietors and ratepayers' of
the district reminding them to pay their Voluntary Assessment of three and
a half pence in the pound to the relief fund.

After Christopher's death in 1856 his widow Ellen ensured that the house
remained a magnet for visitors, particularly poets and writers. Sir Samuel

Ferguson was a friend and regular correspondent, who resisted all her attempts to persuade him of the errors of his Protestant ways. His widow, in *Sir Samuel Ferguson in the Ireland of his Day*, records that Ellen Fitz-Simon was a frequent guest at their home, and the Fergusons too at the Fitz-Simon 'mountain home (where) there was ever a welcome for friends and relatives, and countless attractions to draw them there.'

Lady Ferguson describes Ellen as 'an accomplished and charming woman, most engaging in manner ... said to have had more of her father's genius than any of his children.' Ellen wrote a poem in honour of Ferguson, with apologies to Robert Burns, which began 'Sam Ferguson, my friend Sam, when you I first did know, My locks were like the berry brown, that now are white as snow.'

She wrote constantly – poems, plays, accounts of numerous visits, mainly to Rome and various Catholic shrines across Europe. She spoke and wrote French, and her voluminous papers in the National Library suggest she also knew Spanish, Italian and German. She published a volume of poetry *Derrynane in 1832 and Other Poems* and two other volumes were printed privately. In 1880 she wrote a sonnet, entitled *Glencullen in 1819*, recalling her first walk along 'Glencullen's mountain pathways' on 'a day of breezes, soft and bright, radiant with sunshine', then refreshed with shower, and of her sixty-one years of happy life 'in this beloved spot'.

Other topics moved her to verse. In 1870, *The Prussians occupying the Palace of Versailles* deplored '... the vandals in Versailles, in that proud pile, the fourteenth Louis' sacred monument'. This was not a distant view of a reported event – Ellen, on one of her many continental trips, had found herself trapped in the besieged Paris by the Prussian army.

She seems not to have been moved to poetry by dramatic events much closer to hand. On 6 March 1867, a column of about fifty armed Fenians, bearing a green flag 'got up in very handsome style' bearing the legend 'God and your country – Remember Emmet' laid siege to the barracks in Glencullen, beside the gates to Glencullen House. The five constables refused to surrender. After an exchange of volleys the attackers, according to the correspondent of the London *Times*, said they would place nine policemen they had earlier taken prisoner in front of their lines if the defenders did not yield.

The besieged constables eventually promised to surrender on condition the prisoners were freed. It was agreed that this would be done, but only after two hours, and the attackers left, heading for Kilakee, and eventually Tallaght, taking with them all the guns and ammunition they found in the barracks.

A decade after Ellen O'Connell's death another aspiring poet had his first poem published. He was John Millington Synge, and his poem, which appeared in the Trinity College journal *Kottabos* in 1893, was entitled 'Glencullen'. Synge was a regular visitor to Glencullen, usually on his bicycle, and often with his sweetheart, the actress Molly Allgood. His letters to Molly, and others, have many references to it. On 20 July 1906 he wrote to Molly, 'I had a long ride today up by the lower end of Glencullen and Kilternan. It was a very beautiful day with a wonderful lustre in the sky and a clear blue sea...'

Later that year, on 16 October, he wrote to Molly, 'I've been hard at work all day – except of course for my outing, when I came in for a big shower in Glencullen and got soaked to the skin.' The following February, already ill with the cancer that was to kill him, he wrote to Molly saying, 'Dearest Heart, Great deal better, but staying in bed still. Infinitely depressed, infinitely weary... This day four weeks we had our last walk. Do you remember in Glencullen where we sat on top of the bank? I wonder when I'll be about again.'

One week later, to Molly, 'I think now the cold is gone, I'll soon be well, and we can go off and see how Glencullen is.' He died in March 1909, and one of his last published poems was entitled *In Glencullen*. In it he addresses the song birds of Glencullen, and warns them to beware of the kestrel and the roving gun, finally admitting:

> You great-great grandchildren
> Of birds I've listened to,
> I think I robbed your ancestors
> When I was young as you.

A few years later another poet found his way to Glencullen. He was the Belfast-born Joseph Campbell, who returned from a time in London in 1911 to live with his new wife Nancy in a cottage in Dundrum. A political activist as well as a poet, he is today best remembered as the author of *The Gilly of Christ*, and, at another level, of the lyrics of *My Lagan Love*. It seems he moved up to Glencullen soon after arriving in Dundrum, for the archive of W.B. Yeats letters shows Yeats writing to Campbell, mostly on matters

Glencullen

Left: O'Connell's Rock.

Below: The stone in front of Glencullen House marking the engagement of Christopher Fitz-Simon to Ellen O'Connell in 1824.

relating to the Abbey Theatre, in 1911, with the letters addressed to Joseph Campbell, Glencullen, Kilternan, Co. Dublin. Another letter is dated 1915, by which time Campbell was apparently living in Glencullen House, probably as a tenant. The address this time is 'Glencullen, near Rathfarham'.

Campbell's mark on Glencullen's history was, however, more political than poetic. In 1914, it is reported that he, along with The O'Rahilly, addressed a meeting in Glencullen to organise a company of the Irish Volunteers. The following year, according to one report, he 'lent' the lawn of Glencullen House to men of Connolly's Citizen's Army for drill with rifle and bayonet, and possibly to the women of that army also, for local tradition says Countess Markiewicz visited the house.

But he attracted less militant visitors also. Lilly and Lolly, the sisters of W.B. Yeats, record a Sunday spent at Glencullen House at the invitation of Campbell and his wife, in 1914. The day was fine, and they admired the delightfully old and rambling house, and the wonderful views of the Sugar Loaf from its garden. After the visit, one of the sisters had a visitation of sorts – Lilly, as sometimes happened, found herself transported into the past and into the mind of another, in this case that of Ellen O'Connell.

Their other brother, Jack B. Yeats, also visited Glencullen House, and his notebooks for this period include two pencil sketches labelled 'Young Campbell, Glencullen House'. They show a young child, presumably the son of Joseph Campbell, in a leafy setting, but neither depicts the house.

At the end of the Great War the house seems to have been empty for several years, with the Fitz-Simon family living in Moreen at Sandyford. In 1920, according to family lore, the barn beside the unoccupied Glencullen house was 'borrowed' by Michael Collins and used by the IRA to manufacture arms. Collins himself, it is said, called at Moreen to tell the family to stay away from Glencullen, until further notice. Presumably the barracks was, by that time, no longer a barracks as it would have been no distance from the barn.

Two years later, during the Civil War, Glencullen again slipped into the annals of history when a party of thirty-one Irregulars plus their motor-car and equipment were taken prisoner by Free State troops in an engagement at Glencullen Bridge in August 1922.

But it was the rambling poet, playwright or artist, rather than the flying column, who most often found his way to Glencullen. In the 1930s Samuel Beckett was writing to a friend to tell him of a long trek to Enniskerry, by way of Glencullen, crossing over Prince William's Seat. His purpose was to disagree with the friend's suggestion that the landscape around Glencullen was 'gardenish'. 'The lowest mountains here terrify me far more than anything I saw in Connemara or Achill,' wrote Beckett. 'I was reduced almost to incontinence by their calm secret hostility. I ran down to Enniskerry.'

When Sam Beckett was roaming around Glencullen the Fitz-Simon family fortunes had declined. In the mid-nineteenth century they had owned extensive property in both Dublin and Wicklow, running to thousands of acres, but by the 1930s most of the land had gone. Glencullen House itself, on twenty-six acres, was sold, and passed out of Fitz-Simon ownership for the first time. Even then it continued to add modestly to its historic and artistic pedigree, for it was purchased, in about 1940, by the Irish-American sculptor Andrew O'Connor, now best remembered for his Triple Cross on the sea front at Dún Laoghaire, but aptly too for his statue of that earlier habitué of Glencullen House, Daniel O'Connell, which is now in the Dublin City Gallery.

Presumably not wishing to leave Glencullen entirely in the hands of O'Connell and Michael Collins, Dev got in on the act, or at least local memory has him making his way up to a snow-bound Glencullen in the fierce winter of early 1947. Heavy snow in February made the road to Glencullen impassable, and the valley was cut off, with reports of cattle and sheep dying for want of fodder. The story is that the then Taoiseach tramped up on a pair of antiquated snow-shoes. Of all the pictures conjured up for me by Glencullen's rich historic tapestry, none quite matches that of the tall, austere De Valera making a stately progress up the hill on a pair of snow-shoes. Where on earth did he get them?

Our patchwork knowledge of Glencullen's history took all of our twenty years there to acquire. Some of it we came by accidentally, some by following up local gossip, but much of it from the man who bought Glencullen House back into the family ownership in 1953, Lt. Col. Christopher Richard Daniel Manners O'Connell Fitz-Simon MC, or simply 'The Colonel', as we came to know him shortly after moving into 'Whin Cottage'.

Seven

The Colonel

Our introduction to the Big House was suitably genteel. Our friends Jimmy and Eleanor Tobias, who lived down at the bottom of the glen, were already on good terms with Colonel Fitz-Simon and his wife, who was a Belfast-born Protestant. Mrs Fitz-Simon, we learned, was unwell, a semi-invalid in fact, and unable to read with any comfort. Eleanor was going in to read to her on a regular basis, and had suggested to Mrs Fitz-Simon that my wife Katherine might be willing to do so too. So Katherine was invited over.

My own introduction to the Colonel could well have been earlier and sharper; he was, at that time, still driving a far from new Austin A40. Whether from habit, absent mindedness, the almost total lack of traffic on Barrack Road, or a residual sense of *droit de seigneur,* it was his custom to cruise serenely out through the Grand Gates and onto the road without pause, hesitation or sideways glance. Once or twice already he had frightened the life out of me, but I had managed, so far, to avoid a collision. Fortunately he decided shortly after we arrived that his driving days were over.

Sadly Mrs Fitz-Simon died before Katherine had a chance to read to her, and the Colonel was left on his own with only his sheepdog Lassie for company and daily visits from Mollie, his housekeeper. Once he gave up the motorcar he was, not house-bound for he walked a lot, but Glencullen-bound, and was happy to accept any offers of lifts to shops or opticians or other necessities, and eager, too, for company and conversation.

He had been born in Glencullen House in 1898, and had grown up there, and in Moreen at Sandyford, before going to Sandhurst and then joining the Leinster Regiment. When we got to know him he had three passions in life: Glencullen House (or Glancullen, he insisted on using the old pronunciation); his O'Connell ancestry; and the British Army, in particular the Leinsters.

He had served in France during the Great War, getting wounded, and winning the Military Cross in 1918, and also in the Second World War, in India and Egypt in the King's Own Royal Regiment (the Leinsters having been disbanded in 1922).

Buying back Glencullen House in 1953 was probably a romantic, and quixotic, act of homage to the O'Connell-Fitz-Simon heritage. When he bought it in about 1940 Andrew O'Connor had renovated it, improved the plumbing, and installed electricity which was generated on site. But in 1953 it must still have needed massive expenditure, and the Colonel, I think, was far from a wealthy man.

Some of his first moves were back, not forward. He removed the electric lights from the dining room where O'Connell in 1823 had first proposed the founding of the Catholic Association, and he had somehow rescued the original dining table. A very formidable Ellen O'Connell-Fitz-Simon still dominated the room, looking proprietorial in a large oil portrait over the mantelpiece.

We have a treasured memory of dinner by candlelight in that room, at that table, with the Colonel and his younger son Nick, home from Australia with his family, with Ellen over the fireplace, and the ghost of Dan loitering in the corner near the dumb-waiter. The ghost of the Liberator had to share the house with the Leinsters and other reminders of British Army life – a regimental drum hung in the stair well.

The Colonel's first visit over to 'Whin Cottage' was on a winter day with a sharp wind scything up the valley. I was pottering around the garden when he marched down the driveway. Remarking on the turn in the weather he told me he had decided it was cold enough to wear George's coat. I had no idea who George was, or why the Colonel was wearing his coat. It transpired that George was King George, and the coat was the Colonel's old army one. I was never sure which George it was, V or VI, or in which war he had worn it.

Thereafter, he was a regular visitor, not on a near daily basis like Sean the Postman, but every now and again, and always at Christmas, usually on St Stephen's Day morning. The welcoming cup of tea – or 'mug o tay' as he called it – was often his tipple, but so too was a glass of sherry. I think he would have

Glencullen House, *c.* 1975.

Colonel Manners O'Connell Fitz-Simon with Glencullen House in the background *c.* 1983.

The Colonel, *c.* 1968. Photo courtesy of
Christopher Fitz-Simon.

preferred whiskey, but, unlike him, we were not great whiskey drinkers.

On his Christmas visit he always brought a bottle of sherry for Katherine, and we usually gave him a bottle of wine. One year I was in Brussels the week before Christmas, and coming home through Brussels Airport I noticed a special promotional sale of whiskey in the duty-free. I knew very little about whiskey, but recognised the Johnny Walker label at an attractive price, and bought one.

We gift-wrapped the Johnny Walker and put it under the Christmas tree. On Stephen's morning the Colonel arrived and, before settling down in front of the fire with a glass, produced the usual bottle of sherry from the pocket of George's coat and presented it to Katherine. I went over to the tree to pick up the gift-wrapped bottle for the Colonel, but paused as he began to tell us he had had a nice surprise that morning.

Christopher, his elder son, had called up early, he told us, and presented him with a bottle of whiskey.

'And damn fine whiskey it was', he continued. 'None of your old Johnny

Walker rubbish, but real quality Scotch.'

I excused myself and went into the kitchen, grabbed the first bottle of red wine I could find, and hurriedly wrapped it. The Johnny Walker lived with us for some time, but I hesitated to serve it to guests.

The Colonel had *The Irish Times* delivered daily and was an avid reader, particularly of world news. He followed my reports from places like India, Hong Kong or Japan with particular interest – Japan because he himself had narrowly missed fighting the Japanese on India's eastern border in the Second World War, and because many of his colleagues and friends had suffered horribly as prisoners at the hands of the Japanese. He could never understand my enthusiasm for all things Japanese, and my accounts of the unfailing courtesy and politeness one encountered in Tokyo.

One summer, a close personal friend of mine, a Japanese journalist I had known in America and also on my regular visits to Tokyo, came to stay with us for a few days in 'Whin Cottage'. I told the Colonel that Kiyoshi was coming, and that I would bring him over to visit Glencullen House on Saturday afternoon.

'I don't want to see him. I do not like the Japanese and I cannot forgive them for what they did to my comrades.'

'Look', I said, 'Kiyoshi was still a boy when the war ended, and he very nearly died in the fire bombing of Tokyo. He's no more a fan of Tojo and the militarists than you are, and I think it would do you good to see him, so I'm bringing him over, and I hope you will be polite to him.'

So we wandered across the field to Glencullen House on the Saturday afternoon, Kiyoshi clutching a bottle of Suntory whiskey I had suggested might be a suitable peace offering. As I expected, the Colonel was politeness itself, and talked cheerfully about his time in India, and carefully about his colleagues who had been taken prisoner. Kiyoshi was fascinated, by both the man and the house.

It was another week before I saw the Colonel again. 'Well, I said, what did you think of my Japanese friend?' 'Seemed a nice fellow,' he admitted grudgingly, 'I still don't like the Japanese. But they make damned good whiskey.'

The Colonel, while very much alive to current affairs, both international and local, was also, for me, a wonderful bridge to a past world. He talked sparingly about his experiences in two World Wars, usually only in response to questions, or when something particularly reminded him of a past event. Something I had been reading led me, as we sat chatting one afternoon, to mention to him the truce of July 1921, between Lloyd George and De Valera.

'Oh yes,' he said 'I remember that day well. I was lying reading a book in the sun on the lawn outside some old schloss that we, the Leinsters, were billeted in, in southern Germany, or was it Austria. Suddenly all hell broke out in the lines – great banging of drums, shouting and singing. I wandered over and asked what was going on. "They've given us our freedom, Sir." the soldiers told me. 'The British, they've given us our freedom. We just got the news." That was how I heard of the truce. They were a bit premature in their interpretation of it, but near enough, as it turned out.'

When *The Irish Times* sent me to India for a two-week trip, the Colonel wanted to hear all about it on my return. He himself had loved India, and at the end of the war had served in a high position with the Indian railway police. I mentioned that I had been to Kerala, in the south. Yes, he said, he remembered it well. There were some lovely beaches there, and one in particular where the branch line ran right alongside it. He and the Memhsaab had a private train at their disposal and they loved to park it at the beach and go for a swim. My trip to India suddenly sounded very pedestrian.

Another day the conversation turned to horse-riding, and I recounted how, in Ethiopia, I had had my own horse, and how it had been possible to ride for miles in open mountain countryside. This prompted a recollection by the Colonel, not of cavalry exploits in the Great War, but of a marathon ride from Glencullen to the other side of the Phoenix Park to join a hunt with the Meath Harriers, all because he had taken a great fancy to a young lady member of that hunt, hacking fourteen miles there and back, with a day's hunting in between.

Not everyone in Glencullen took to the Colonel. Some of the more Republican-minded thought they were forwarding the cause of national freedom by pointedly refusing to refer to him, or address him, as 'Colonel', sticking to 'Mr Fitz-Simon'. They could not dismiss a mass-going Catholic and direct descendant of Daniel O'Connell as a west Brit and foreign invader, but neither could they ignore his service in the British army.

I too, at first, found him a bit of an enigma, but soon came to appreciate just how wonderfully the Colonel himself, and Glencullen House, embodied the great contradictions at the heart of modern Irish Nationalism, or rather how, by being totally oblivious to those contradictions, both the man and the house showed how nonsensical was the twentieth-century definition of Irishness almost totally in terms of non-Britishness.

On my very first visit to him in Glencullen House, he was sitting in the very agreeable library room, with its comfortable couches, bookshelves and door out to what had once been a tennis court, reading a volume of James Morris' *Pax Britannica* trilogy on the British Empire. He told me how good it was, and how I simply must read it. Some years later, when speculation was mounting in the newspapers over the future of Hong Kong, and it was being suggested that Britain would hand the colony back to China, he greeted me as I walked into the library with a question, 'What on earth are we doing with Hong Kong?'

I was puzzled by this, and replied with a question, 'What do you mean by "we"? We are not doing anything with it. None of our business.'

'Oh come on,' he replied, 'You know what I mean – we British, the British – are we just going to walk away from it?'

To him there was no problem being the proud descendant of the Liberator, unquestionably Irish, but also being British. He regarded my question as a piece of hair-splitting. Another afternoon I had called over to give him a lift in to see his doctor, and was browsing among the bookshelves in the library while he was getting ready. As regards books, the library was a big disappointment. The original house collection had long been dispersed, and most of the shelves held modern novels, book club editions and the like.

But one volume did catch my eye, it was a hard back, and it turned out to be a privately printed 1863 edition of Ellen O'Connell's *Derrynane and other Poems*. Two poems stood out; one was entitled 'To the Queen, June 1837', and began:

> Fair Queen, we greet thee
> With blessings and smiles.
> Thou art the hope
> And the pride of these isles.

It was a tribute addressed to Victoria on her accession to the throne, 'Called now to reign/ O'er the mightiest empire/ The world doth contain…', and its final verse expressed Ellen's, and Ireland's, hopes for the reign then commencing,

> For reform made complete
> England looks up to thee.
> And Scotland expects

A like blessing to see:
While Ireland, long wronged,
In the dawn of thy reign
Sees the day star of hope
Rise triumphant again.

The second poem was entitled 'To the Queen; December 1861' and was written on the death of Prince Albert, as one widow to another. It begins,

God Save the Queen
No flatterer am I,
But from my heart I breathe that earnest prayer,
For sure it is a thing of all most rare,
Such good to find
In one was born so high …

Appended to the 1831 poem in this 1863 edition is a note which says the lines,

are the heartfelt expression of the author's feelings towards the Queen who had but just ascended the throne, and among whose first acts was one of justice and kindness to Ireland. The author sees with pleasure and pride that although evil advisers may since have, to some degree, lessened the Queen's regard for this country, yet that upon the whole Her Majesty's career has amply justified the expectations which are expressed of her.

Sitting reading these lines by Daniel O'Connell's daughter, in a room no doubt frequently graced by O'Connell himself, I had to rethink my stereotyped view of O'Connell, and remember that he was never a separatist, and remained all his life a monarchist.

In a later browse around the library I found another unusual book. This again was a privately printed volume, an autobiography by John Clarke MacDermott, Minister in the Unionist Government of Northern Ireland during the Second World War, long-serving Lord Chief Justice of Northern Ireland, and finally Lord of Appeal in London. The explanation for its presence in what was almost a shrine to Daniel O'Connell was that MacDermott was related to the Colonel by marriage, being a cousin, of some remove, of Mrs Fitz-Simon, as indeed, I learned, was Tyrone Guthrie.

My musings on these strange interweavings in the fabric of Irish history were given added spice when I read John Clarke MacDermott's account of a day out in Dublin as a young student.

He and his brother had gone on a day excursion by train from Belfast to Dublin; the day was Easter Monday 1916. Arriving at Amiens Street station they had headed up to O'Connell Street and across into Henry Street, presumably going to see the Four Courts, Dublin Castle and the older part of the city. Somewhere beyond Mary Street they became aware of a general disturbance in the city, and asking what was going on, were advised to get back to the station as soon as possible, as there was word that the trains might not be running.

They hurried back along Mary Street and Henry Street, noticing as they passed that some windows had been broken in the G.P.O. and there seemed to be a lot of activity inside the building. So they pressed on and got a train back to Belfast, little realising how close they had come to involvement in one of the most dramatic days of modern Irish history.

As the years passed, we saw more and more of the Colonel. He gladly accepted Katherine's offer to drive him on shopping trips to Bray, and on occasional excursions to doctors, opticians, hearing-aid experts and the like. He and I enjoyed each other's company, and I spent many Saturday afternoons chatting with him in the library, or, when the weather was cold, in a little study he retreated to. We saw more of the house; the inevitable 'mug o' tay' was made and served in the large basement kitchen; Katherine and I would hold our breath as the Colonel lifted the large kettle of boiling water from the stove and directed a steaming stream roughly in the direction of the waiting pot. He never missed.

The kitchen was only part of the basement; there were other rooms filled with boxes, piles of books and bits of furniture. One cellar held the instruments of the long defunct Glencullen Silver Band. In days gone by, we learned, the band had entertained spectators at matches of the Glencullen cricket team on the lawn in front of the house. There was no cricket in Glencullen in the 1970s, but the village still boasted a dedicated tug-of-war team, and the modestly named Gaelic football team, the Glencullen All Stars.

As the Colonel became more frail, so did the house. There were problems with the roof, and the plumbing was turbulent. I found myself called upon to ascend ladders and replace odd slates, and tackle other jobs. Late one Christmas Eve, with the Glencullen weather displaying its full complement of cold, wind and rain, we got a telephoned cry for help from the Colonel. The rain was pouring in through the roof and threatening to bring down the ceiling of the pump room – the pump room was the main way in and out of the house from the yard at the side, and still contained the pump that had once been used to lift the water supply from the well to the tank above.

When I got there, accompanied by my schoolboy son, part of the ceiling had already come down. From the amount of water pouring through it looked much more like a burst pipe than a leaking roof. The Colonel said all the pipes fed out of the large tank above the pump room, so I suggested we cut off the supply to the broken pipe, and he could get a plumber in after Christmas.

Up the ladder I went, clutching a torch, and through the trap door opening into the icy blackness of the roof space. I found the tank, but cutting off the supply was not straightforward. The flash lamp picked out half a dozen pipes coming out of the sides of the large tank and disappearing off into the darkness, and there was no clue as to which one had the burst. The size of the tank was another problem; it was about chest height, so by stretching upright and leaning over the rim I could just about survey the dark pool below. The flickering beam soon showed me that there were more than six outlets from the tank, one or two above the water level, the rest, as far as I could see, inches below the surface.

Hanging from the rim of the tank on bits of string were roughly cut wooden pegs; one or two more were floating on the surface of the water. It dawned on me that these were the high tech means of cutting off the flow to individual outlets; all I had to do was reach down and shove one into each pipe opening in turn, and when the cascade below dried up, I would have found the culprit. The trouble was that the surface of the water was out of my reach, never mind the actual holes.

So I rolled up my sleeves, hoisted myself up, and balancing face-down on the edge of the tank, reached down into the icy water and shoved one of the wooden plugs into the nearest hole. A shouted negative from the Colonel below answered my query as to whether the water had stopped. I tried another hole, without success. As I stretched further across towards the next candidate and into the wet darkness below I realised I was in imminent danger of overbalancing and plunging headfirst into the tank. So I summoned my son up the ladder, and got him to hang on to my feet as I went over the top.

After another ten minutes or so, just when I was chilled to the bone and my arms from the elbow down had gone totally numb, a roar from the Colonel below told me I had found the leaking pipe and staunched the flow. When I clambered down the ladder I found him grinning broadly and trying not to laugh; my son had just given him an account of my gymnastic plumbing technique and the picture of me hanging almost upside down in the dark up to my elbows in icy water, plus the fact that the leak had stopped, had cheered him up enormously. He insisted I have a glass of whiskey, and for once, I accepted. He was still chortling when he came over on Stephen's Day morning.

Though the house was a constant worry to him, and his own health was failing, he never let the ageing process depress him too much. One day I found him in high good humour, and asked him why. The chiropodist had visited him that morning, and he recounted an exchange with him. There was some problem with his foot, to do with a toe, I think, and he had read somewhere that this sort of thing could be dealt with by means of an operation to amputate the toe.

He asked the chiropodist would he not just chop it off for him. The chiropodist was a man of very few words and not at all a bundle of laughs. He said nothing, stared morosely at the Colonel's foot for a minute or two. 'How old are you?' 'Eighty-two' said the Colonel. 'Hardly worth it.' replied the chiropodist. The Colonel had found this uproariously funny, not least because the chiropodist had shown not a flicker of a smile, or indeed any lessening of his silent and Stygian demeanour.

The Colonel died fourteen years after we had bought 'Whin Cottage'. Without him, Glencullen was, for us, a duller place.

Eight

The Irish Times

The Irish Times, when I joined it, was, a bit like Glencullen House, a ram-shackle amalgam of many strands of Irish life and history. But even in 1968 it was far from the bastion of Anglo-Irish, West British Protestantism that many still continued to label it, though it did house some reminders and relics of old times. The typewriters, for which we had to compete on a daily basis, looked as though some of them might have predated the end of British rule.

One Sunday morning a year or so after I joined, I had to collect something from the office in Fleet Street and took my three-year-old son in with me. It was Diarmuid's first visit and he gazed round the large almost deserted news room, with its vast desks.

'Look, Daddy,' he cried in amazement, 'Look at all the tripewriters.' It was a profundity which delighted one of the few people present, Eileen O'Brien, and duly found its way into her *Irishwoman's Diary*. Eileen, Irish-speaker and Belfast Republican was as far from a West Brit as one could imagine. George Burrows, on the other hand, was from Malahide, and would have seemed to many the perfect embodiment of the Five per Cent, the well-to-do Protestant minority. To me he was the kindly figure behind the rich plumy tones I had grown up with in Lisburn, listening to the Topical Talks that followed Athlone's lunch time news.

Another familiar voice that now took human form was that of Lionel Fleming, whose refined Cork accent had, for years, conveyed the world scene with insight and a measure of dry humour to legions of listeners to the BBC's Home Service, where he had been Diplomatic Correspondent.

Michael Viney, whom I had met some years earlier in Belfast, was not a West Brit, but a true Brit who had left a career in journalism in London to move to Ireland, and ended up in *The Irish Times* where he was a specialist feature writer. He brought with him, in addition to his English accent and very English manners, a fresh view of Irish life, society and politics which some might have decried as naïve, but which in practice enabled him to produce excellent series of articles embodying an invaluably detached analysis of aspects of Irish affairs in the 1960s. These were well-researched and comprehensive, covering topics such as the place of the Protestant minority, divorce, adoption, illegitimacy, and they were key factors in moving *The Irish Times* to the forefront of journalism in what was becoming a new Ireland.

I was later to become good friends with two rising men at that time, who personified the close relationship that had existed between Trinity College and *The Irish Times* – Andrew Whittaker, and Fergus Pyle. Both were Trinity graduates, as indeed was the editor, Douglas Gageby, and his deputy, Bruce Williamson. Another Trinity man was Terence de Vere White, from a family background as Catholic as it was Protestant. As Literary Editor he had also, I think, the status of Assistant Editor. He was precise, even precious, but I found him a delight to work with. I knew he was a writer, and had read one of his novels before I ever went to Dublin, but to my regret it was not until years later, after his death, that I read his autobiographical *The Fretful Midge* (1957) and found it one of the wittiest and best accounts of Ireland in the 1940s and '50s.

But the people I worked with most closely in those early days were far from Trinity types. Dónal Foley, the news editor, was a gregarious Gael, and graduate, not of Trinity College, but of the emigrants' boat, various labouring jobs, the London Midland and Scottish Railway and odd-job journalism.

His long-suffering, paper-clip chewing assistant was Gerry Mulvey from Tyrone, from a prominent Nationalist family, who had learnt his journalism in provincial newspapers. He was as conscientious and neurotic as Dónal was reckless, chaotic and easy-going all at the same time. His assistant in turn was another Northerner, Dan Duffy, from the slopes of Binevenagh in north Derry, also a long-time graduate of provincial journalism, and as lovely a man as one could wish to meet. These two, Gerry and Dan, while deep-died Northern Nationalists, had long accepted the myth that Northerners, compared to their Southern brethren, were hard working and totally reliable, and that Northern Protestants were doubly so. So they welcomed my arrival as a gift from heaven.

Heaven and allied regions were the bailiwick at that time of John Horgan, the Religious Affairs Correspondent, graduate of the National University not Trinity, fresh from Vatican Two, and rapidly adding to the work of Viney in building the paper's credentials in serious journalism. An old friend from undergraduate days and Irish history student congresses, Owen Dudley Edwards, learning that I was joining *The Irish Times*, told me I had to look out for Horgan, who was a 'sound man' and was certain to be the first Catholic editor of the paper. Owen was right on the first if wrong on the second, though John had the compensation of being in turn a Senator, a TD, an MEP, a professor and, in the end, Press Ombudsman. He was to be my closest friend in the paper in those early years.

He should have had honourable mention in the saga of 'Whin Cottage', for not only did he lend a hand with some of the hard labour at the outset, he was also the channel for an interest-free loan of what, to me, was a handsome sum of money, which helped ensure that we moved in to something that was one or two stages beyond a building site, and allowed us the luxury of owning our very first washing machine, a twin-tub and a marvel to watch in action as it vibrated its way around the kitchen floor.

A contribution to the establishment at 'Whin Cottage' also came from another helpful friend in those early days – Dick Walsh. This took the form, not of hard cash, but of a cat, the redoubtable Sooty, a beautiful black and white moggy of good if mixed pedigree who lorded it over the house and its occupants, animal and human, for the next decade.

The Irish Times, during working hours, was an extremely social sort of place. 'Old Foley' as he became affectionately known, though he was far from old, presided over the open newsroom from 'the desk', combining work with much banter and chat from mid-morning until the 5p.m. editorial conference, after which he presided over the Pearl Bar, a convenient ten yards or so across Fleet Street, where he was joined by reporters who were just finishing the 'day' shift, by reporters who were on their way in to the 'evening' shift, by sub-editors who 'had just slipped out', by journalists from RTE or other papers, by visiting 'firemen' and by an array of (mostly) entertaining citizens who were either connected to *The Irish Times* in some mystical way, or who just fancied the company of journalists.

Despite his dishevelled appearance and at times shambolic approach to order and organisation, Old Foley was somehow the focus around which the daily work of the paper revolved. Most of us loved him, and loved working for someone who so obviously enjoyed his job, and thought everyone else should too. But there were other serious souls who muttered that Foley was a chancer, and wondered how he got away with it.

Gageby was different. He was not just the editor, or 'the boss' – he *was* the *Irish Times*. It was his paper, and one could not help feeling that we were there just to help him bring it out every day. I cannot recall ever seeing him in The Pearl. He was a bit like an old-style landlord, and we were the tenantry who had the privilege of working the estate. Not that he was autocratic or stand-offish; he was a very benevolent landlord, on the friendliest terms with the peasantry, often coming out of his office to chat with this one or that one, always addressing us by our first names, offering generous praise for work well done.

In some ways his was a very democratic regime. His office, which at that time he shared with Bruce Williamson and a secretary, was directly off the newsroom, and his door was indeed open to anyone who wanted to see him. The main news conference at five in the afternoon, held in his office, had anything between a dozen and eighteen staff members at it. In later years he instituted what he called a 'shout in', when he would call all the editorial staff to the newsroom and, perched on a chair, preside over a totally open discussion on anything and everything to do with the paper.

But he had a temper. Every now and again he would begin a conference by throwing the previous day's paper on his desk and declaring it to be '★★★★ing awful'. We all felt guilty; senior executives would shuffle their feet and stare at the floor. On occasions he would single out an individual for a barrack-room dressing down – it might be the Picture Editor, even a Deputy Editor. It was not pleasant to see senior professional people humiliated in front of their younger colleagues, even if they had dropped a clanger.

Such events were infrequent, but they served to remind us all that he ran the paper. There was no real hierarchy; we were all equal, and equally fallible, under Gageby. It may be the only way to run a newspaper, with one sure hand on the tiller, and an easy, affable approach that generates team spirit and loyalty, with behind it the threat of the lash.

In my early days I was surprised and delighted by Douglas's friendliness and encouragement. In five years of working for another great editor, Jack

Sayers at the *Belfast Telegraph*, where I ended up as his Chief Leader-Writer, I never once had lunch with him, and we were never on first name terms. Douglas remembered my photograph of Slemish, for which he had paid me three guineas many years earlier, and he loved talking about County Antrim, about Slemish, about Donegore and about Belfast. Sometimes this was over lunch at his modest retreat, the RIAC Club on Dawson Street, sometimes with his old army pals in the mess at McKee Barracks. These invitations did not mean I was a particular favourite – sometimes they included other reporters, and others, I know, were similarly treated.

When I joined in 1968 I was, like Douglas, an enthusiastic supporter of the Civil Rights movement in the North, and was happy to be working on a newspaper with such an interest in, and policy on, Northern Ireland. I knew Douglas had started journalism with the strongly Fianna Fáil *Irish Press* group, working closely with its boss, Major Vivion De Valera, of that ilk, but if I thought at all about that, it was to wonder how he had ever fitted in there, not how on earth he had come from there to running *The Irish Times*. My first inkling that stronger views lay behind his romantic zeal for all things Northern came over an article I wrote on Lord Brookeborough, in the autumn of 1968.

Douglas had asked me to do a series of interviews with the older genera-tion of Northern politicians – people like Eddie McAteer, Harry Diamond, Betty Sinclair, Cahir Healy, and, of course Brookeborough. I rang Colebroke, in Fermanagh, where Brookeborough was living in baronial retirement, and was invited to the house. I had met him only once before, though I had often seen him in operation in the Stormont House of Commons, so I was expecting the haughty and rather cold individual which had always been his public persona. The long drive up to the rather bleak but imposing por-tico of Colebroke heightened such anticipation.

Far from it; the man himself greeted me cheerfully at the front door, dressed in baggy corduroys and a rough tweed jacket. He whisked me into a small morning room just off the great entrance hall, invited me to sit down and offered tea. The room opened directly through French windows onto a garden, and from there emerged the formidable figure of Cynthia, Lady Brookeborough, armed with a garden fork and basket.

'Don't mind me,' she said addressing me 'I'll just be popping in and out to the garden.'

The interview was going well, and Brookeborough seemed happy enough to answer questions on anything from his reaction to 1916 to current agitation over discrimination against Catholics. Lady B.'s forays back and forth had become quite frequent, and she seemed to linger longer in the room each time, until at one point she intervened to say,

'Basil, don't answer that. I know what he's getting at, I can see what he wants you to say.' To which Basil replied, 'Now, now dear, it's perfectly all right, you get on with your gardening.' He then turned to me and said 'Sorry about that. What was it you were saying?' and proceeded to answer the question.

It was a good interview, subsequently much quoted, but Douglas did not like my first draft, and made me rewrite the intro and take out some short passages. What he objected to was my contrasting of the stern public image of Brookeborough with the charming gentleman who had so freely answered all my questions. To Douglas, Brookeborough was a figure to be hated, not humanised.

To him the true Ulsterman was the Northern Protestant who had joined Wolfe Tone in the United Irishmen in '98, and he doggedly clung to the belief that, under the layers of Orangeism and bigotry that had swept over the province since, such real Republicanism could still be found, and revived, in Protestant hearts. His heroes, his holy trinity, were Tone, Armour of Ballymoney, and Bulmer Hobson, though Armour had never been more than a Home Ruler, never a separatist let alone a Republican. He earned his place, however, by having been both a Home Ruler and a Presbyterian Minister, and by being based in north Antrim, which had earlier been one of the heartlands of the United Irishmen in 1798.

Hobson, now almost forgotten, was among the leaders of Irish Republicanism in the era before 1916, and was, I think, Douglas' particular hero. Like the other two members of the trinity, he was a Protestant Nationalist, but he was also an Irish language enthusiast, active in the Gaelic Athletic Association, and a founding member, and later secretary of the Irish Volunteers. He was undoubtedly Northern – born in Holywood, educated at Friends School in Lisburn. His Quaker connection did not prevent him writing, in 1909, *Defence of Warfare: A Handbook for Irish Nationalists*, nor stop him supporting armed force, though he opposed the idea of an open rebellion such as the 1916 Rising, and retired from revolutionary activity after it. As Douglas once said of his own father-in-law Sean Lester, Hobson learned 'that the gun was not the answer'.

Hobson gained further merit in Douglas's eyes by having spent much of his life in printing and journalism, founding and editing two Republican newspapers. He had also written a biography of Tone. There was a personal connection too – Hobson was a lifelong friend of the Lesters, and Douglas would have met him frequently in their company. Lester was another Northern Protestant who had gone in for journalism and militant Irish Nationalism, and later gained celebrity as the last secretary general of the League of Nations. Douglas shared one other passion with his hero Hobson – both were mad about trees.

Once I became Diplomatic Correspondent and the EEC entry negotiations began in 1970, my work in the paper rarely touched on Northern Ireland. That did not stop me writing about it, as Michael Viney was constantly looking for short feature articles for a slot he edited on the leader page. As the crisis deepened through 1971 and 1972, I became increasingly aware that my views on it were not those of the editorial line of the paper or of the editor himself, particularly as, by then, Douglas had enlarged his heroic trinity to include John Hume.

We argued from time to time over the North, but, up to then, never quarrelled. He grinned and bore it when I turned iconoclastic at an editorial conference and suggested that we might raise the quality of our leaders if we lowered the Tone. He even laughed when, in response to a bit of banter started by Old Foley on what sort of names we might have for condoms if and when they were legalised in Ireland, I suggested 'Armour of Ballymoney'.

But we had one real row, late in 1972. I had written somewhere, not for *The Irish Times*, a short parable comparing the 'national question' to a dispute over a small piece of land in rural Ireland. One old bachelor farmer (the South), who had long cast envious eyes on the fields of a neighbouring holding (the North), decided his best chance was to marry the elderly neighbour's daughter, pension off the father, and unite the two farms.

He put it to the father (London), who was not too keen, but said it was up to the daughter. The daughter said no way was she marrying that scruffy old scarecrow without a penny to his name, and why would she. The farmer replied that it made sense; the farms belonged together, and should never have been separated. She was being totally unreasonable, he said, anyone with any wit could see that it was the right thing to do. He told the father he should make her marry him.

Another neighbour suggested that if he had a shave, bought a new hat and coat, tidied up the farm, and tried wooing the neighbour's daughter, he might have more chance of success. But he said there was nothing wrong with him as he was, he was more than good enough for that girl, and she would damn well have to marry him.

At that time Dublin was strongly supporting the Nationalist demand for a British 'declaration of intent' regarding the reunification of Ireland, and *The Irish Times* was giving its editorial backing to it. I had the idea of enlarging on my parable, and expanding the theme of it into a detailed examination of how both policy and public opinion in the Republic regarding Northern Ireland were falling into the same errors as our farmer. I decided to use quotations from recent *Irish Times* editorials to illustrate the argument, and produced not one but three pieces, citing misguided pearls from our leading articles as the framework upon which they hung.

I offered them to Michael Viney and he took them off to read them, coming back to say he thought they were great, and he would use them asap. I was off in Brussels for several days, and returned to be met by a much chastened Viney who told me Douglas had pulled the first article from the paper when he read it in the page proof, had bawled him out, and was now gunning for me. Remaking a feature page late on the day of production was a rare and very bothersome thing to have to do.

I went in to see Douglas and we had our first and only real row. He did not lose his temper – his rage had been against Viney for putting the offending article into the paper more than against me for writing it – but told me in, for him, reasonably restrained language, that it was completely unacceptable for a senior journalist on a newspaper to use the pages of the paper to demolish that paper's editorial policy in such a manner.

I had to concede he had a point, and I offered to rewrite the articles removing all reference to *The Irish Times*. I could do what I liked, he said, but if I felt that strongly about the *Irish Times*' editorial policy, then perhaps I should think of working somewhere else. Instead of taking that hint, over the next few days I sat down and reworked the articles reducing them to two, not three. I then handed them directly to Douglas, who muttered and said he would take a look at them.

A day or two later, I asked him about the articles. Oh, he replied, he had forgotten about them, but he would have a look. About a week later I asked him again; he looked blank and said he must have lost them. I said no problem, I had copies, and handed them into him. Another week passed before the articles appeared, on consecutive days, not on any feature page, but at the back of the paper on what was an overspill news page on big-paper days; they were clearly labelled 'a personal view'.

Douglas passed no comment. The incident put him up in my estimation, not down; he had, probably justifiably, been outraged at my attempted public dissection of the paper's editorial line, and he personally disagreed with, and intensely disliked the arguments I put forward in the revised version. But he was too good an editor to let this mean the paper could reflect only his personal views.

Just how he reacted to a letter to the editor published a few days later, I can only guess. It read as follows:

Sir, - As a regular (and regularly depressed) reader of your confused and disingenuous leading articles on the Northern situation, and of the myopic effusions of most of your correspondents on the same subject, I hasten to congratulate you on the publication of Dennis Kennedy's admirable article 'Prescription for Disaster'.

Sooner or later Irishmen will have to realise the absurdity of the twin myths that 'partition' is maintained by 'British imperialism' and that it could be ended by British pressure on the Northern majority; in the meantime is it too much to hope that Mr. Kennedy might be allowed to take over the writing of your leading articles on this complex and difficult subject?

Yours, etc.,
J.W.Gray, M.A., F.R.Hist.S. Cranmore Avenue, Belfast.

J.W.Gray had lectured me, most eruditely, on Medieval British History at Queen's University. I had last seen him on my graduation day in 1958. Bruce Williamson must have been selecting the letters for publication that day.

Relations were fraught for a few weeks in 1972, and I was glad each evening to escape to Glencullen, and put Fleet Street out of sight and out of mind.

Nine

The 44B

Escape to Glencullen was, more often than not, by means of the 44B bus. This was, for the select few who knew about it, the star in CIE's firmament, every journey rich in adventure, drama, and mystery, and not a few visited by misfortune. A single decker, it made a handful of round trips daily from central Dublin out to Glencullen. Its city centre berth was in Poolbeg Street – it later migrated round the corner to Hawkins Street - and its ultimate destination was away up in the mountain wastes of Ballybrack above Glencullen.

For a time after moving into 'Whin Cottage' we tried to run two cars. In those days driving into Dublin was no great problem, but it was becoming expensive, and we soon realised we simply could not afford the second motor, so unless I was working the late shift, I had to rely on public transport.

Thus began a long and meaningful relationship with the 44B, usually in its 18.45 manifestation ex Poolbeg Street or Hawkins Street. Getting in to the office was reasonably simple; there was a lift in with Jimmy Tobias if I wanted it, and Katherine could always drop me down to Kilternan to get the 44 from Enniskerry, a regular, reliable double-decker service totally lacking in the character and temperament of the 44B. Getting home was the real problem, and that was where the 44B played its crucial role.

Its terminus was about a two-minute sprint from the second-floor newsroom of *The Irish Times* in Fleet Street. The sprint was essential, because the last 44B from town to Glencullen was the 18.45, and the early shift in the paper ended at 18.30, or thereabouts, or whenever you finished what you were doing. The 44B kept potential passengers on their toes. Every now and then, but not very often, it would actually leave at 18.45. More often it was closer to seven o'clock, sometimes later, once or twice nearer to eight o'clock, and often enough, never at all.

It seems the 44B was somewhere near the bottom of CIE's priority list, and it was not unusual for an inspector to arrive at about 19.15 to inform a truculent knot of travellers that a bus had broken down in Stoneybatter, and the knock-on effect was that he had no idea when he was going to find one for Glencullen.

There was little one could do, except complain, and take the next 44 and walk the three miles up from Kilternan, all of which could add hours to the journey home. At times like that one looked around the knot of stranded passengers, hoping against hope that Ena Cotter was among them. Ena was the wife of John Cotter, that is Big John, not Little Johnny, the Human JCB. Big John was as silent as Little Johnny was loquacious. Both had come to Dublin from Cork years earlier, to work on the turf during the Emergency, otherwise know as the Second World War, and both had stayed. Big John had married Ena, the genuine Dublin article from the inner north city around Sheriff Street, and shortly after we settled into 'Whin Cottage' they bought the old forge from Jack Flanagan, and Big John set about transforming it into a small palace.

If he was given to silence, Ena was not, and she had a voice, accent and vocabulary to be marvelled at. I have seen a mature CIE Inspector take to his heels and run from Hawkins Street as Ena informed him, and the whole street, what she thought of CIE, of the poor man himself, and of the class of buses they expected decent people to travel in, when they could find them. Once or twice it seemed to work, as a bus would shamefacedly creep round the corner after a beleaguered and abused Inspector had gabbled a distress signal into his walkie-talkie. But generally it just made the rest of us feel better, as we worked out how we would get home.

Non-appearance of the bus was not the only hazard. It was not unknown for the 44B to break down; once or twice it actually got lost, and there was always the possibility of prolonged immobility on the narrow winding mountain road that constituted the final phase of the journey. This would happen when the bus met an oncoming car, lorry or tractor with a particularly obdurate individual at its wheel who was just too pigheaded to give way, or who was not aware of the rule of the road, which was that the bus gave way to no one, and anyway had no reverse gear. The experienced 44B driver in this situation would normally switch off his engine, take the *Evening Herald* from his hip pocket and settle down for a quiet read. Passengers would then calculate how far they were from their particular stop, and decide whether it might be quicker to walk.

As the last four or five miles of the journey were on a road barely wide enough for the bus itself, this was a daily, or nightly, possibility. The route to Glencullen was normal enough out southwards through Ranelagh, Milltown, and Dundrum – the main route that led eventually to Enniskerry. But above Dundrum the 44B turned sharp right at Lamb's Cross, then took an almost hairpin left at the Lamb Doyle's, and followed the boreen across the face of the mountain through Barnacullia and Ballyedmunduff to Glencullen.

One dark winter night we regulars were dozing quietly as an almost full bus struggled up the hill beyond Dundrum. Fortunately not everyone was asleep, for the driver, not a regular on the route, was cheerfully speeding past Lamb's Cross when a shout from behind told him to stop, he was on the wrong road, and should have turned right. He, and the conductor who was also new to the route, were inclined to dispute this but there was a clear majority against them, so he manoeuvred back to Lamb's Cross and set off on the proper course. There were voices aplenty to warn him to turn left at the Lamb Doyle's, though when he saw the laneway he was being urged to enter, he thought his leg was being pulled, and he took some persuasion to proceed. Thereafter he needed repeated reassurance that he was indeed on an authorised CIE bus route. How he ever got back to Dublin with no passengers to guide him remains a mystery.

In my time as a regular we had several breakdowns; twice we simply had to abandon ship and hike off on our own, as the driver could promise neither a repair team nor a replacement bus. Once, when a rather elderly bus could not make it up one of the steeper hills, we had to disembark and walk up the hill, until the poor bus, wheezing heavily, eventually joined us. At least we were spared the indignity of having to push.

But such adversities served only to make us appreciate even more the joys and delights of the 44B when it ran smoothly. The Ring of Kerry is a boring marathon compared to the reckless sprint of the 44B on a summer evening across the face of the Three Rock Mountain, then up the shoulder of the Two Rock, with the whole of Dublin Bay spread out below to the left, and eventually, up the Khyber Pass and over the 1,000-foot contour line. (The Khyber Pass so named because that bit of road was cut when the north-west Frontier was grabbing the headlines.) At that point the Bay disappears, the city with all its botherations is left behind, out of sight and out of mind, and the entirely rural prospect is of Glencullen below and the mass of the Wicklow Mountains ahead.

This Nirvana is reserved for the privileged few, for by then most of the passengers have been deposited at the Blue Light, the small pub in Barnacullia, or in Ballyedmonduff, or elsewhere along the road, and only the handful destined for Glencullen itself are still on board. If the journey has been a hazardous one, they share something of the Hillary-Tensing sense of achievement. This is particularly true in winter, in high winds and driving rain. With an uninhibited young driver at the wheel, the 44B buckets and bounces along the mountain road with the rain lashing the windows. Dozing passengers catching glimpses down below of the lights of Dublin and Dún Laoghaire have mistakenly imagined they were on a jumbo jet making a turbulent descent to Dublin airport.

Such experiences generate a strong camaraderie among the regulars. You could sense this once you passed Dundrum; most of the faces were familiar, many were well known to each other. The crowd who boarded at Dundrum heading for an evening's music and drinking in the Blue Light or Fox's added to the sense more of an outing than a daily commute. For a time in the seventies the Blue Light outshone Johnny Fox's as a haven for thirsty musicians. One fellow who regularly got on in Dundrum would take his seat at the back of the bus and produce a harmonica, which he would play expertly, non-stop, until the globe of the Blue Light summoned him.

The Blue Light had high standards in those days; it is said the management once asked a couple of aspiring musicians to give it a rest as the customers were unimpressed by the efforts of component parts of the future U2.

On some rare occasions both the camaraderie of the bus and the atmosphere of drowsy familiarity were rudely fractured by a dispute among the passengers. Old animosities can linger for years among country people, and who knows when or why they erupt. Anyway, one night the usual crowd got on in Dundrum, and the bus was almost full. Before long some remarks were passed between two men near the back; one was a truculent fellow with masses of black hair, who was taking no cheek from an older man a few seats up.

Suddenly the pair of them were out of their seats and at each other. The young conductor thought of intervening, then thought again and called on the driver to stop. The driver stopped, as did the fighting. As captain of the craft and man of authority, the driver marched down to the back and lectured the two men on their behaviour. As a precaution he ordered the older man to move up to a vacant seat at the front, and we moved off. A couple of minutes later the black-haired devil leapt out of his seat, dashed up the aisle and landed a cuff round the ears to the other fellow. Combat was renewed. The driver came to a sudden halt, which propelled the entangled adversaries in a heap right to the front of the bus.

In some odd permutation of limbs, one leg with a heavy boot on the end soared upwards and smashed the driver's rear-view mirror. This assault on public property sobered the two, enraged the driver and brought murmurs of disapproval from the rest of us. By now the driver had had enough; he ordered the black-haired one off the bus, and the other man to the back of the bus. The black-haired man tried to argue, but was ushered, and pushed by the driver down the steps and off the bus, into the inky darkness.

He looked around and declared 'But this isn't my stop,' and clambered back up the steps. Faced with this reasonable argument, the driver let him back on again, shoved him into the seat at the front recently vacated by the enemy, and told him not to budge until we reached his stop. And that was that.

The 44B was, for me, a useful vehicle for getting to know my neighbours better, and for catching up on all the news about them. Some of them worked in Dundrum, and were regulars on the bus. Anyone who had gone into Dublin for shopping or anything else, had to get the 18.45 if he or she wanted home that night.

One evening I rushed round to Poolbeg Street and grabbed a seat as the bus was leaving. I found myself sitting beside a very nattily dressed Jack Flanagan, from whom I had bought 'Whin Cottage' a few years earlier. I had not seen him for some time, but I knew he had married and was living across the valley towards Enniskerry. I hardly recognised the clean-shaven gentleman in the soft hat, so changed was he from the unshaven, roughly-dressed stone cutter with whom I had bargained for 'Whin Cottage'. We had a long chat and he mentioned he was doing some work in town and would be a regular on the bus. When we reached the crossroads at Glencullen, his wife was waiting for him in the car, and gave me a lift down the road.

A few days later I bumped into Johnny Cotter, fount of all local gossip, and told him I had met Jack on the bus, and he was looking very grand. 'Oh yes, sure he's the head man now at the Bank of Ireland,' said Johnny. I looked blank, and struggled with the idea of Jack presiding over the world of high finance, so I asked Johnny what exactly he was doing. 'He's the boss down in College Green. He's over all the work they're doing down there. Sisk has the contract.' Then the truth dawned; Jack, expert stone cutter that he was, had been appointed foreman at the restoration work on the old Parliament Building, the Bank's historic headquarters. Sisk owned the quarry in Glencullen and was supplying and working the granite and Portland stone needed for the job, and the stonecutters.

I sometimes had difficulty bridging the gap that separated my two worlds of Glencullen and *The Irish Times* office in Dublin 2.

Ten

Points of Departure

The eccentricities of the 44B had implications far beyond anything you might imagine. They affected my relations with Douglas Gageby; they may well have influenced *Irish Times* policy on significant issues; academic theses in far places bear their faint imprint.

As Diplomatic Correspondent I was expected to write leaders – leading articles, or editorials. Unlike other newspapers I knew, such as the *Belfast Telegraph*, *The Irish Times* had no officer class of specialist leader-writers. Instead, leaders were generally written by senior reporters who had been designated to cover selected areas – the Political Correspondent, the Education Correspondent, the Industrial Relations, Religious Affairs or Diplomatic Correspondents. As these were the individuals with special knowledge who would have written the stories which seemed to merit editorial comment on the day, it was a sensible arrangement, but it could also mean that writing the leader was an extra chore added on to the end of a day's work.

Nor did *The Irish Times* have anything resembling the formal daily 'leader conference' which I had met elsewhere, in which the editor and his closest associates discussed likely topics, decided the line to be taken, and assigned subjects to writers. Instead, at the end of the main news conference as people were beginning to leave his office, Douglas might remark that he would write a note on such and such and ask if anyone else had something in mind. Or he might suggest to Bruce that China was worth a look, or East

Timor, or Brazil. (Bruce Williamson, as well as Deputy Editor and Letters Editor, was the nearest thing we had to a regular leader writer, almost always on foreign topics.)

It was all very casual, but people would volunteer leaders, anxious, perhaps, to stop less informed colleagues blundering into their area, or simply because they had something to say. I can remember no serious argument over any line to be taken, or indeed much general discussion of the likely content.

The 44B came into serious play, if, when I was on the day shift, Douglas would suddenly decide at about six o'clock that we should, after all, have a leader on some aspect of European affairs, or indeed simply ask me to come up with a topic and a leader. Forty minutes or less is no great time to find a subject, research it, think about it, decide what to say, phrase it in the authoritative but never pompous prose style favoured for *Irish Times* leaders, and present it to the editor for his approval. The possibility that the 44B might be running to schedule and was already belching diesel fumes round in Poolbeg Street certainly concentrated the mind, and may even have, on occasions been the deciding factor in preferring the line first thought of to any other that might have emerged after prolonged soul-searching.

Years later I was approached by an earnest Austrian student who was doing a doctoral thesis on Irish policy towards European integration in those years when I was writing practically every relevant *Irish Times* leading article. I was a bit alarmed when he told me he was using *Irish Times* editorials as one of, if not *the* primary source for this thesis. I thought it wiser not to tell him too much about the circumstances under which they were written, and I am happy to say he did become Herr Doktor, and something of an authority on the subject.

This seemingly casual attitude towards editorial comment reflected Douglas' own view that an editorial could not be, and should not try to be, a learned treatise on its subject, nor a profound analysis of policy – that way lay pomposity. It was, instead, a short and sharp reaction to and comment on a news item of the day. Its purpose was to stimulate some thought and reaction; if it could also amuse, so much the better.

It gradually dawned on me that Douglas took a certain pleasure in landing me with a leader just as my thoughts were turning to Poolbeg Street rather than Brussels. As I got to know him better I realised that what annoyed him was the idea of any journalist rushing to get away from the office just as the journalistic day was taking off. Early shift and late shift meant nothing to him; he liked to be in the office when the paper went to bed, and usually stayed until the presses began to roll and the first pristine copies came off.

He sometimes, but not always, looked into the office in the morning – the noon news conference was more often than not taken by Donal Foley. He preferred to take the main afternoon conference himself, and stayed on to write a leader, or to approve those written by others. But he almost always went home for dinner, coming back towards eleven to see the last stages of putting the paper together.

Later, when I had the job several times a week of being in charge and editing the paper late at night, I understood his enthusiasm for being there in person. In those days of hot metal and all the craft associated with printing in the pre-computer age, there was a wonderful air of excitement shared with a team that included type-setters, sub-editors, other production staff, all working flat out to meet a series of deadlines while the rest of Dublin was either in bed or straggling home from the pub.

Nothing could compare with the great roar of the presses as they came alive, or of the nightly miracle of the appearance off them of the crisp new copies of the first edition – something entirely new, created almost from scratch over the past twenty-four hours. Beautiful.

Douglas loved that moment, and loved the people he shared it with, no matter what their status. The journalists who were still around at that moment, mostly sub-editors, were, to him, real journalists, unlike those who rushed off to catch a suburban bus at 18.45. It never occurred to him that the numbers present were unusually large, or that many of them were there mainly to collect a free copy of the new paper, having timed their journey home from the Pearl Bar or some other pub with that in mind. The more cynical were probably there because they knew it did them no harm at all in the eyes of their editor.

Douglas always had a rather soft spot for sub-editors, perhaps because almost all his own journalistic career had been at an editorial desk rather than out on the street as a reporter. No long-serving reporter could have had such a charitable view of the sub-editor species. He began in 1945, straight out of the Army, as a sub on the *Irish Press*, and by 1949 had risen to be *Assistant Editor* on the new *Sunday Press*, thereafter being in succession editor-in-chief of the *Irish News Agency*, Editor of the *Evening Press*, and from 1963 on, editor of the *Irish Times*.

He also had excellent relationships with the printing side, the real workers who set the type, made up the pages, cast the moulds and operated the presses. They in turn had the greatest regard for him, not least because he always knew what he wanted and could make instant decisions on 'boxing out' – adding to the print run at the last minute – or holding an edition, and risk missing the Cork or the Galway or wherever train, in order to change the front page.

The more I worked with him, the more I appreciated some of his qualities as an editor. He took the letters page very seriously, and while others edited that page, he often grabbed a pile of unedited letters to see what they contained. There was an unwritten rule that, when a running controversy developed, the letters published should be in direct proportion to the letters received in terms of sides taken. Letters openly and articulately critical of the paper itself, or any of its writers, were almost guaranteed publication. And staff members who felt wounded or misrepresented by any letter that appeared and wanted to reply would be discouraged. 'You've had your say already, now it's the readers' turn', was Douglas's usual comment.

In some ways the Letters Page was the glory of the paper in those days. Unlike many other newspapers, readers' letters were given generous space and prominence. It, more than almost any other page, reflected the individuality of the paper, its own peculiar quirkiness. Where else but on the Letters Page of the strongly anti-apartheid *Irish Times* could you have read a response to a statement from the Irish Anti-Apartheid Movement beginning with 'The drums are beating again down in the kraal at Barton Road East…' The reference was to the home, in Churchtown, of Kadar and Louise Asmal, the leaders of the Movement, and its official address. That particular letter writer, a Mr R P Edwards, invariably described the Anti-Apartheid HQ as 'the kraal in Barton Road East'.

In the spring of 1970 the most serious problem troubling the readers of *The Irish Times* was not the upcoming negotiations on EEC membership, nor the threatened national bank strike, but the wording of the ballad 'She moved through the fair'. For several months the Letters Page was swamped by contending schools as to the correct version.

Douglas did not approve of members of staff getting their pictures, or those of their relatives, in the paper. He was furious when, years later, not at my request, a picture appeared of me in my full doctorial canonicals at a Trinity graduation.

I admired and envied his ability to deal with problems on the spot. His policy regarding errors in the paper was simple – if we got it wrong, we held our hand up and said sorry. When a furious letter would come directly to him to complain about something in the paper, he would tell his secretary to get X on the phone immediately. The outraged party would be told by the secretary that Mr Gageby the editor of *The Irish Times* wanted a word with him, and Douglas would bark breezily down the phone 'Gageby here, I gather we've annoyed you. What's the problem?'

Nine times out of ten the outraged party would be so impressed that the editor of *The Irish Times* had taken the trouble to phone him personally, and promptly, that his ruffled feathers were instantly smooth, and he almost ended up apologising for taking up the editor's time.

He was also ready to receive visiting lobbyists and delegations who wanted to make a case to him. He himself did not play the man about town. He was rarely, if ever, to be seen at receptions or public dinners, but if people wanted to come in and talk to him, that was fine. When the Troubles erupted, all sorts came down from the North to Dublin, and a session in Gageby's office was on most of their agendas. John Hume called regularly, as did Maurice Hayes and Roy Bradford, and I was usually asked to join in the chats. Other posses were dodgy enough, and I realised later that after leaving us they might well have gone on to Leinster House to ask for guns, or for money for guns.

In the early seventies, as the paper flourished and advertising increased rapidly, Douglas would regularly remark at an editorial conference that we needed more space for news and if we could not add pages, then some columns of advertising would have to be held out. To us this sounded like a wholly admirable exercise of journalistic primacy over the grubby commercialism of advertising. It confirmed our view that we journalists were the real paper, and that Douglas was in total control. He certainly never deferred to the representatives of non-editorial departments who attended our conferences, and was often enough dismissive or downright rude to people from advertising, circulation or promotions.

But of course he was not in total control. He was the editor, but Major Thomas Bleakley McDowell was the Chairman and Managing Director and the ultimate controlling authority. To most of us journalists he was a name often heard, but the man himself rarely seen, except perhaps fleetingly as he slipped into his office in the D'Olier Street side of the building. I had been two or three years Diplomatic Correspondent of *The Irish Times* before

I even met him, and that was by accident when he introduced himself to me at a reception at Glencairn, the British Ambassador's residence.

He was a very hands-on chairman, in the office everyday, with a finger on every pulse and an eye on us all. Douglas was for ever scurrying down the stairs 'to see McDowell' and made no secret of his admiration for him both as a company lawyer and as a manager.

He played the military man, always using his British military title, dressing in pin-stripe with furled umbrella, at one time using a monocle, and running his office like a command post, staffed almost entirely, as far as I could see, by men. He had a black London taxicab to ferry him around. He had the most alarming habit of fluffing up his generous moustache by putting the back of both fists up to it, shaking them vigorously and blowing out at the same time. One of his 'men' logged in all visitors to his office, and out again – '10a.m., Kennedy in: 10.10a.m., Kennedy out' – though I am sure the twenty-four-hour clock was used. The same with all phone calls.

When car phones first came into use, the Major was greatly taken by them, and he had one installed in each of four or five cars used by the top managers on the commercial side of the house, linked to a command centre back at the office. The phones were designated 'Paper 1', 'Paper 2' and so on, and the car-driver was instructed to identify himself as such when using the phone. Part of the idea was to enable the Major to get in touch immediately with key personnel in case of any emergency.

These details were gleefully related to me one day by Donal Foley, as, bursting with laughter, he came up the stairs from the Major's bunker. He had overheard the Major using the new system to summon up the production manager with the words 'Control here; come in Paper 2, come in Paper 2, where are you', and eliciting the reply 'How're ye Major, Jim here, I'm just coming down through Swords.' To which the Major, or was it Control, had snapped 'You are Paper 2, Paper 2. How often do I have to tell you?'

Many jokes were told about him, but he was no joke. He effectively 'owned' *The Irish Times* for three decades. When I joined in 1968 he was Managing Director, and ownership still rested with the Board made up of five or six individuals, all Protestant, who had taken over from the Arnotts, and kept the paper going at a loss until first McDowell and then Gageby had been brought in to modernise it and make it a paying proposition. Once the paper was sold into the new Trust in 1974, he was in total control, as Chairman and inventor of the Trust.

Decades later, in 2003, much was made of McDowell's dealings with the British Ambassador in Dublin in 1969, and with the Foreign Office. The Ambassador, the bagpipe-playing Scot, Sir Andrew Gilchrist, was as much a period-piece as McDowell. He had come to Dublin in 1966 on a pre-retirement posting, having spent much of his career bearing the white man's burden in places such as Thailand, Morocco, India, Singapore and Indonesia.

The papers released under the thirty-year rule included a letter from Gilchrist to the Foreign Office dated 2 October 1969, in which he said he had lunch with McDowell that day, and McDowell had told him that he and his 'associates' (presumably the other board members) were increasingly concerned about the line *The Irish Times* was taking on the Northern question under its present editor. Gilchrist reported McDowell as saying that Gageby was a very fine journalist and an excellent man, but 'on Northern questions a renegade or white nigger.'

The immediate row following the release of the papers focused on the use of the phrase 'white nigger'. While I had no problem believing that McDowell was unhappy with the line Douglas was taking on the erupting Northern situation, and that he might well have expressed such sentiments over lunch to Gilchrist, the phrase seemed to me to be straight out of the vocabulary of Gilchrist, not of McDowell. It was simply not the sort of language McDowell would have used.

But the papers released were about more than that. The lunch of 2 October had arisen out of an earlier approach by McDowell to the authorities in London, including to Number 10 Downing Street, expressing a desire to help, and, according to Gilchrist, saying that a certain amount of guidance 'in respect of which lines were helpful and which unhelpful, might be acceptable.' John Martin, in his 2008 *The Irish Times: Past and Present* gives a detailed account of the whole affair, and argues that it is clear McDowell 'wished to place the *Irish Times* under the influence of the British State' at that critical time. Some alleged that McDowell was working for MI5.

McDowell's response to the controversy in 2003 was to say that his only interest at the time was to help solve the problems of Northern Ireland, and to ask Downing Street if 'the Irish Times Ltd' could contribute towards a peaceful and satisfactory outcome. At one point he had suggested that *The Irish Times* (presumably the limited company rather than the newspaper) might bring together prominent people from North and South in an informal forum or conference.

At the time none of this was common knowledge to us reporters on the paper. Some of the most senior journalists, such as Bruce Williamson and Ken Gray, may have been aware, as I was later to be, that McDowell, along with other members of the Board, was unhappy with Gageby's strong Nationalist line on Northern Ireland, but they almost certainly knew nothing of the contacts with London.

How sinister was all this? No journalist likes to admit it, but under western capitalism newspapers are owned by their owners, not the people who write them. The Board, i.e. the owners, of *The Irish Times,* we now know, were, in October 1969, unhappy with the line their newspaper was taking on the most dangerous crisis the island had faced since the Second World War. What could they do?

They could have sacked the editor and appointed a new one to take a different line. That they did not do so suggests they were not sufficiently unhappy with his line, or they realised that to do so might have been commercially disastrous for the paper, and might have contributed nothing to a peaceful resolution. McDowell himself had a finely tuned (or greatly exaggerated) sense of public duty, both his own personal one, and that of *The Irish Times,* as can be seen in the archaic wording of that oddest of documents, very much his document, the Memorandum of Association of the Irish Times Trust, and he may well have wished to see the entity, the Irish Times Ltd, making a positive contribution to offset, in part, the unfortunate line taken in the pages of the paper.

It has been suggested that these insights into events in 1969 tell us why Gageby abruptly vacated the editor's chair in 1974; that he was, in fact, eased out by McDowell, who by then had taken over total control of the company. I find this hard to believe. When the Board made Gageby editor in 1963 they knew all about his Nationalist views, and his strong links to the broad Fianna Fáil family. They made him editor, not just in the hope that he would make the paper profitable, but in the knowledge that he would remove from it the vestiges of it being the paper of a small Protestant minority. It had already ceased to be a Unionist paper.

What they had not anticipated was that their rapidly improving and ever more important paper would be confronted with the challenge of reporting, analysing and dissecting a crisis of the magnitude of that which engulfed the island and its politics from 1969 on. In those circumstances Gageby's Nationalism was something of an embarrassment to them, but there was little they could do about it, short of sacking him, which they were not prepared to do.

That crisis, if indeed there was a crisis, passed. But the problem arising when a happy relationship between owner and valued editor is suddenly upset by unprecedented events or circumstances must have been much in McDowell's mind when he drafted the Articles of Association that were to govern *The Irish Times* from 1974 on. Under these 'the editorial policy to be followed by the Irish Times shall be as decided by the Directors from time to time and they shall ensure that it is in conformity with the objects of the Company.'

The prospect of having to work under such specific direction as to editorial policy may not have appealed to Douglas Gageby in 1974, and may have been one factor in his sudden decision to retire. But he was happy enough to return three years later under the same conditions, and resume his uniquely successful partnership with the Major.

McDowell, despite his appearance and affected manner, and his undoubted eccentricity, was no West British relic. His background was ordinary Ulster rather than Anglo-Irish, with an overlay of British military. But he was essentially paternalistic in his attitude towards *The Irish Times*. He took an unnerving interest in the journalists who wrote the paper, knowing every little detail about them, even those whom he had never met. Douglas probably told him all about my unhealthy preoccupation with the 44B.

Eleven

Stormy Nights

Escape on the 44B from stormy exchanges in Fleet Street did not mean that Glencullen was always a haven of peace and shelter. We found, soon after we moved in, that our decision to raise the roof by four feet when we were rebuilding 'Whin Cottage' might have been a bit hasty. The cottage lay on an axis from north-east at the upper end, to south-west at the lower, and the sharp fall in the land meant that the lower gable reared up to a considerable height.

That gable housed our master bedroom, with a small window in the end and a larger one at the front. It also took the full brunt of the south-westerly gales that seemed to blow most of the winter, and more than occasionally at other seasons. This was not what we had planned. We had known that the prevailing wind in any part of Ireland was from the south-west, but our gable looked directly onto the massive wall of Glencullen Mountain topped by Prince William's Seat, which constituted the southern boundary of the glen at that point, and effectively blocked off the south-western approach to 'Whin Cottage'.

So we built our windbreak of conifers at the top of the garden, from where, on a very clear winter day, you could just make out the peaks of Snowdonia, and from where, we were advised, cruelly cold easterly gales might be expected. The conifers flourished, and still do to this day, but were never needed as a windbreak. For whatever topographical reason, the easterly gales skipped over or slipped round 'Whin Cottage'.

Not so the south-westerlies, which seemed determined to remove the cottage entirely. Our first high wind from that quarter, in our first month, introduced us to a sound the memory of which still unnerves me. It was a rhythmic pounding, beginning immediately above our heads as we lay in bed, which increased to a crescendo, then died away in the distance. It was a bit like an angry giant rattling an enormous club along a set of railings.

In fact it was the wind getting under the heavy concrete interlocking tiles that formed our roof and lifting them just enough to create a snake-like ripple the length of the roof, slamming them down again as it went. It sounded as though the roof was suffering severe damage, but when I crept out early the next morning, to my surprise and relief I found it intact.

We came to dread south-westerly gales. Sleep was impossible, not least because of the irregular pattern of the assaults on our gable end. Lying awake during a lull, we could hear the wind grumbling to itself in the bottom of the valley, organising its forces for the next attack, then we could hear it gathering strength before hurling itself against the gable and wrestling ferociously to get under the tiles. After that all would be quiet for several minutes, apart from the rumbling discontent at the bottom of the valley.

The strongest gale of that first year removed three tiles. Cringing under the blankets we heard them go, skipping and thumping across the roof. We found them smashed on the driveway up to the gate, and were relieved that only the three had gone. We thought we had lost half the roof.

We consulted a local builder friend, who told us the mountain barrier we thought would shelter us was making things worse. Like a stone wall round a garden, it meant the wind simply accumulated against the blockage before spilling over it with increased and outraged ferocity. That, he said, was why a hedge or some conifers made a far better garden windbreak than a wall. More helpfully he said that the tiles on our roof should have been nailed down, not left to rely on their own considerable weight to hold them in place. So he did a job on the roof, nailing down every third row.

That helped, but not a lot. We felt a little more secure, but the wind still found plenty of tiles to get under, and the sleepless nights continued. Then we had a real storm, a howling gale, exceptional even by Glencullen stand-ards. It set about the systematic demolition of 'Whin Cottage'. We knew it was going to be a rough night when, around midnight, we heard the first tiles skipping off towards Wales. Then there was a crash of falling masonry and shattering slates.

I wrapped myself up in a coat and went down to investigate. In the darkness and driving rain I could see what had happened. Attached to 'Whin Cottage', and marching down the hill below it were, in turn, the old original cottage which was now a shed, and below it the low lean-to building we called the piggery. This had a corrugated iron roof, sloping up to the gable end of the old cottage.

The wind had taken the sloping tin roof, rafters and all, and slammed it upright on its axis flat against the gable end of the old cottage. The impact had demolished the chimney stack in the gable, which had then smashed down through the slate roof, leaving a gaping hole. The wind, seeing the opening, had streamed through the hole and blown out the window in the cottage, frame and all, and had taken the rickety door off its hinges. The dog had taken to its heels and was nowhere to be seen.

There was nothing I could do but go back to bed, pull the blankets over my head, and try to count the tiles as they skipped and bumped off into the night. In the morning I found fourteen of them, some smashed, several whole, including one a field and a half away. It had flown more than a hundred yards.

That morning the Colonel stumped over to see what damage we might have suffered. He said he had several trees down in his driveway, and because of this he had come over the field by the Ballycog Gate. I had never heard of the Ballycog Gate; it turned out to be the seldom used farm gate in the estate wall of Glencullen House just across the road below 'Whin Cottage'. I asked him where the name had come from, and he said he had no idea, it was always called that, after the townland on which our cottage had been built.

After he had gone I got out an Irish dictionary and looked up 'cog'. The nearest I could find was 'coch', which was near enough. It means a sudden gust of wind, or a squall. If my knowledge of Irish had been greater, I might have thought twice about buying 'Whin Cottage', or at least about adding four feet to its stature. For a time after that we thought of renaming it 'Windy Cottage'.

That stormy night led, eventually, to the reconstruction of the piggery as a garage, and the demolition and grand rebuilding of the old cottage into an extension to 'Whin Cottage', giving us a new kitchen, a downstairs shower and loo, and a long loft under the eaves.

But that was far in the future. Immediate repairs included more extensive nailing down of roof tiles, so we never again experienced any comparable damage, though the wind still kept us awake, marshalling its forces down by the river before hurling itself against our gable end. The roof rattled, but stayed with us. The wind had to satisfy itself with taking items like our incinerator bin and depositing them a quarter of a mile up the road.

Wind was not the only way nature had of reminding us of our temerity in taking on life in Glencullen. But unlike the wind, the snow had its compensations. We got lots of it, and when it came it transformed Glencullen into a wonderland of unbelievable beauty. We were several times snowed in, with no traffic in or out of Glencullen, but this never lasted too long, and while it did we could go sledging in the Colonel's field, or build snowmen, or just marvel at the beauty of everything, happy in the knowledge that we could go nowhere – not to work, or to school, or shopping – and that down below in the slush of Dublin, people were worried and concerned about us and full of sympathy for our plight.

Heavy snow was fine so long as the phone worked and the electricity stayed on, particularly the electricity, as that was needed to make the central heating function, and feed the couple of electric fires we had for emergencies. Without electricity we had very little heat in a house that had not heard of insulation. Initially we relied on one open basket grate in the living room. Banked high with turf, coal and logs, it roasted the shins of those crouching closest to it, but made little impression on anything else. Besides, when going full blast, smoke tended to escape from a fissure at the side of the ornamental granite chimney breast.

When we built the extension into the old cottage, I insisted on spending a fortune on a wood-burning stove, ingeniously linked into the oil-fired central heating. It was soon nicknamed Beelzebub, not so much for the fiery heat it emitted, but for the noxious fumes with which it filled the house if the wind was not in its preferred direction. In fact, unless stoked to the maximum, it gave out little enough heat. On a cold winter morning the entire Kennedy family could be observed jostling for position with backs pressed against the front of Beelzebub. It never really did heat the radiators.

Many workman hours were spent on heightening its chimney, on sealing the joint where the chimney emerged through the roof to stop persistent leaks, and on delicate adjustments to persuade the smoke to go up the chimney, not out into the kitchen. We thought all this had been worthwhile when we had the heaviest snowfall of our sojourn in 'Whin Cottage' in the early eighties. We had three or four feet in the garden, stacked up to more than six feet at the gate. On the first evening the electricity failed.

Beelzebub was stoked to the full, and the kitchen glowed with heat while in the rest of the house the temperature plunged. Our older son had been visiting friends in Rathfarnham, and was snowed out rather than in. The rest of us gathered sleeping bags and duvets and prepared to spend the night on the kitchen floor. Beelzebub must have seen us coming, for before we could settle down, he had filled the kitchen with choking wood smoke; we had to quench the fire, open the kitchen windows wide, and retreat into the freezing interior of the house. Since then that phrase 'wood-burning stove', usually intended to convey all that is best, most comfortable and beautiful about country life, is to me a snare and an abomination.

After a day and a half of total isolation, a snowplough fought its way up as far as Fox's Pub and the cross-roads. That still left more than a quarter of a mile of very deep snow between us and a passable road, as we pointed out to some county council workmen we found in Fox's. The next day we heard the snow plough at work nearer hand. After a while we realised we could no longer hear it; we lumbered out through the snow to find that the road from Fox's down to the bend just above 'Whin Cottage' had had a passage cut through. The plough had disappeared, and we still had about thirty yards of snow up to four feet deep to ensure that we would be driving nowhere.

It took another day or two to have that cleared. Being snowed in had lost some of its romance.

Even a slight fall of snow, or a heavy frost, could put Glencullen beyond reach, particularly if you were driving home at three in the morning. The problem was that whether you went up through Stepaside and Ballyedmunduff, or from Kilternan, you had to negotiate long uphill stretches; the secret was never to lose momentum, in other words never to slow down, let alone stop. So you had to hope that there would be no other vehicle on the road, no stray sheep, and no wandering deer.

Because it was a quieter road with almost no houses on it, the more exposed, long continuous hill up from Kilternan was my preferred route in snow or ice. Its upward gradient was unrelenting, with no level or nearly level bits on which lost momentum might be recovered, and right at the top, just before the village, was a wicked little uphill bend that demanded caution. Several times it defeated me, and I was left with wheels spinning, sliding into the ditch in the early hours.

To help avoid such a situation, the Glencullen motorist normally travelled with several concrete blocks, or large hunks of granite, in his boot, to

Winter in Glencullen.

Whin Cottage *c.* 1974.

add ballast and give the downward thrust needed to generate traction. He was also, in winter, never without a spade. This was needed to excavate soil and gravel from the ditch to scatter under the wheels.

These winter hardships made summer all the sweeter in Glencullen. In spring the field in front of us turned brilliant yellow with buttercups and cowslips, fringed with the deeper gold of the whin bushes. The view down the glen and across to the Sugar Loaf never lost its magic. Sometimes in the early morning the valley would be filled with cloud and we would be looking straight across a sea of white to the tip of the Sugar Loaf. At other times a veil of mist would add a ghostly touch, or a thunder cloud a hint of drama. It was a great place for rainbows; time and again we would be entranced by a perfect arc framing the view from one side of the valley to the other.

With two growing children and a dog, good weather, even in winter, meant a walk. We were spoilt for choice; 'Whin Cottage' being sited on a steep hill, the first question was always 'Up the Road?' or 'Down the Road?' The first meant up through the village, perhaps to the ruined church and the old graveyard. Or, on days when it was open, we could go to the library. There was something almost ennobling in being able to walk through beautiful mountain scenery, along a sleepy village road and end up in a well-kept public library.

Or we could go left at the crossroads and up Ballybrack, with the possibility of a diversion down the Firey Lane which had the added attraction of the remains of an old railway line for wagons which once carried granite from quarries down near the river, or further up the road towards the O'Connell Stone and the Pine Forest.

Down the road was an option never undertaken lightly, for it inevitably meant a lung-wrenching hike up the north face of the Devil's Elbow to get home. By way of consolation there was always the chance of a cup of tea or coffee in the Tobias' cottage at the river before commencing the ascent. But we also had the luxury of going neither up the road nor down the road, but taking directly to the fields over our garden fence, and heading down to Rowdlam. A farm track took us across several meadows, over a stream, and into the old rick yard of Rowdlam. This was a ruined cottage, with very low walls and gables, supported by fat buttresses, surrounded by tall trees and what looked like the remains of a vegetable garden. It was a romantic place, made even more so when we learned that it had been burned down years earlier in a fire started when neighbours were warming the bedclothes for a newly married young couple who were about to begin their new life in it. From Rowdlam we could continue on if we wished, and complete a circle by reaching the Kilternan end of the village and coming home by the road.

On days like that, winter gales were bad dreams, almost forgotten, at least until we arrived at the Ballycog gate.

The division of our world into 'Up the Road' or 'Down the Road' came to have far wider application than which way we would turn when we left 'Whin Cottage' for a walk. Our third child, born in 1974, adopted the terminology from his older brother and sister, but applied it much more widely. Thus Bray was 'Down the Road', but Dún Laoghaire was 'Up the Road', because to get to Bray or anywhere in Co. Wicklow the quickest route was down the road via the Devil's Elbow and Enniskerry, while Dún Laoghaire was nearer via Kilternan, which meant up the road and through the village.

I stumbled on this world view one day when I was packing my bags and telling my four-year old that I was going to Japan. He immediately asked if that was 'Up the road' or 'Down the Road'. I laughed and told him Japan was miles away, on the other side of the globe. But he insisted on knowing whether it was 'Up the Road', like Brussels, or 'Down the Road', and the penny dropped; up the road was the way I set out to get to Dublin Airport. So London, and South Africa and New York were all up the road, but France, where we had started going on holidays, was down the road, as that was the way we headed when driving to Rosslare to catch the ferry to Cherbourg. Japan was 'Up the Road'.

Glencullen's winter weather had some unexpected benefits – it brought us closer to our neighbours. When we were cut off by snow, our neighbour up the hill, Jack Mulvey would appear through the drifts carrying milk and other supplies, and offering any help we might need. Jack was a heavily built, red-faced man with a voice like a fog horn. He seemed to divide his time between digging his large garden, and sitting by his fireside smoking his pipe. Any visitor would be welcomed by a blast on the fog horn, audible in the garden of 'Whin Cottage' on a still day. Both our sons, in their time, were frequent visitors to the Mulvey bungalow and had great regard for Jack. It was only later that I learned that his tendency to shout arose from partial deafness – tinnitus brought on by working for years as a stone mason, with the incessant tap-tap of metal on granite constantly ringing in his ears. Quite a few of our neighbours were so afflicted.

The storm damage to our roof and the partial demolition of the adjacent cottage, plus my determination to rebuild it as an extension to 'Whin Cottage', meant Johnny Cotter, the human JCB, was back in action. He first helped me build a garage on the remains of the piggery, with cement blocks and a corrugated roof, and double doors facing the road. We filled in the gap between the doors and the road, cutting away the hedge to make a new entrance.

Johnny worked well, but his expertise began and ended with the long-handled shovel. He could lay blocks, but had never really mastered the spirit level or the plumb-line, so I made a point of always working alongside him when tricky things like walls were on the agenda. We liked him, and enjoyed the lengthy chats over tea in our kitchen which were the invariable precursor to any work actually being done. He was ready to tackle anything, and I could never have managed the extension without him.

We had proceeded well with the work, and were embarking on the gable wall facing down the hill. This was to be a cavity wall of cement blocks, and I had all the materials to hand. I told Johnny we would leave it until my next day off. It was late autumn, and I arrived home the following evening off the 44B at about half past seven, to be told by Katherine that Johnny had been there all afternoon and had put up the gable wall

I grabbed a torch and went up the ladder to see what had been done. The wall was up about six feet, both leaves, and even in the torch light it was obvious it was far from straight; in fact it leaned out at one end, and in at the other. I took a heavy hammer and started demolishing it before the mortar could set. The great thing about Johnny was that he was not sensitive to criticism. When, a day or two later, I told him I had to knock the wall down, he smiled and said it was better to get it straight, and set about helping me to build it again.

Johnny's wife was Gertie, a small gravel-voiced woman who seemed taciturn if not worse when I first met her, calling at her door to ask for Johnny. We met her again some time later, when she was away beyond taciturn. There was a rap at our door one night, and Katherine went to answer it. Sitting at the fireside I could hear a rasping voice announcing 'It's a complaint about yer dog, Mrs Kennedy.' It seemed that Muffin, our amiable and not too bright young semi-Labrador bitch had raided the Cotters' back garden and helped herself to a dozen duck eggs, which Gertie had been hoping to hatch out and raise for the Christmas market.

We were horrified, and offered immediately to pay for the eggs. A week or two later, she was back again with 'a complaint about yer dog'. Muffin had just helped herself to the dozen replacement eggs. I said I would have the dog put down immediately, and I would pay for the eggs. To my surprise Gertie protested strongly, and said she could not bear the thought of the poor dog being put down, could we just not keep a closer eye on her?

Two or three days after that we were all around the fireside, and our younger son was out in the porch. We heard a rap, and the familiar but dreaded 'It's a complaint about yer dog.' We were totally mortified. Then our five year old appeared grinning round the door into the porch, and repeated his perfect imitation of Gertie's dolorous gravel tones. It became his party piece.

Gertie, for all her gruff exterior, was a dog lover, and as soft-hearted as they come. Muffin survived to make further raids. Johnny raised the fence around his garden to six feet, but Muffin, as we witnessed, could clear it in a leap. We whacked her, we tied her up, we filled empty egg shells with mustard and pepper and force-fed her with them, but where ducks eggs were concerned, she was insatiable. I think Gertie went out of production and switched to something else for the Christmas market.

For the trickier parts of my building projects, beyond the ministrations of the long-handled shovel, I turned to John Keeley, who was sexton at Kilternan Parish, and a competent builder. He could do the plumbing and the electrics, and construct a roof that would withstand the winter gales. He had no time for a long-handled shovel man like Johnny, and gave him a wide berth.

But they did have one thing in common. Both were grave-diggers. It was part of John's job as sexton at Kilternan, while Johnny's expertise with the long-handled shovel was regularly called upon to do similar service in Glencullen. 'Whin Cottage' survived both their ministrations, and is still above ground.

Twelve

An Offer I Could Refuse

One day in the late 1970s I received a phone call in the office from a well-spoken Englishman, asking me if he could meet me for lunch, as he was coming to Dublin in connection with a research project on Northern Ireland. By that time visiting academics and journalists seeking briefings and updates on 'the situation' had become something of a minor nuisance, as their first port of call was invariably the *Irish Times* office.

So I asked him a bit more about the research project and what it involved. He said it was a study of how government policy was made, both North and South, the direct and indirect inputs into that process, the role of the media and public opinion, and so forth. He named a research institute in the English midlands as the base for the programme, and hinted that the proposed lunch might be the first of several. I took a phone number and told him I would ring back.

Before I did that, I mentioned his approach to a good friend, much more experienced in these things than I was. Do it, he said, but only if he pays you. These academics are not short of funds, and they will come over here, pick your brains and waste your time, and pay you nothing if they can get away with it.

I then looked up the research institute he had named, found it was reputable, and rang him back. When I said I could meet him for lunch, he sounded so delighted that I had not the brass neck to mention money. So a week later I met him in the restaurant of Bloom's Hotel off Dame Street – an excellent eating spot at that time – and we had a fine lunch.

His questions were fairly general, much as one would have expected from any visiting journalist, and I had no problem answering them to the extent of my own knowledge. At the end of the meal he said he would be coming back to Dublin on a monthly basis, and asked would I be happy to meet him each time for lunch. He would not, he said, expect me to do this for nothing, and there would be a small payment. Saying which he produced a brown envelope – it was brown – from his briefcase, and handed it to me.

I could see no reason to refuse, so pocketed the envelope and said I would see him in a month. When I got back to the office I found I was £50 richer. The envelope contained ten crisp Central Bank of Ireland fivers. Fifty pounds, in the mid-seventies, was still a welcome addition to a journalistic salary, especially when all one did in return was eat a free lunch.

So the monthly lunches continued. I found his company congenial enough, and we talked about lots of things besides his research interest. Each month I left Bloom's Hotel with my stomach nicely full, and ten new Irish fivers in my pocket. He did ask specific questions – did I think John Hume's influence on Dublin Government policy was a key factor? Who was Charlie Haughey's closest advisor on Northern policy? But he never took notes, and he never came with a prepared questionnaire or anything like that.

I was sure each lunch would be the last, as I felt I was giving poor value; anything I told him he could already have read in things I, or other commentators, had written in *The Irish Times* or other Dublin newspapers. After about five such lunches I had a phone call asking me if it was at all possible to meet him in Belfast next time, as he was going to be there, and I might be able to show him around.

That suited me fine, and I met him at the Europa Hotel, and with the help of a journalist friend based in Belfast I took him by car on a tour of Belfast's hotspots – Divis Flats, Ballymurphy, Sandy Row, and East Belfast. My friend dropped us back at the Europa, and in we went for lunch.

This time it was different. After a few pleasantries he looked me in the eye and said 'Dennis, I am sure you realise by now what this is all about.' I almost choked on my smoked eel as I cast desperately around for solid ground. Before I could say anything he told me he was, of course, very familiar with all the places I had shown him that morning, had seen them many times before. He had just wanted me to come to Belfast so we could have this conversation here.

He said he worked for the Foreign Office. The research project was just a front, and they used the institute as a useful contact point. They would like me to work for them. They needed first-hand information on individuals, what they were thinking, what they were doing. I sat in a daze, at first furious that he had made a fool of me, letting me drive him around half of Belfast like a tour guide, telling him lots of stuff he already knew. I was angry, too, that he had let me compromise my journalist friend by involving him in this charade.

All I could say was that this was a total surprise to me, that I had assumed I was helping him with an academic research project, and that I had no idea I was getting into anything as devious as he was suggesting. He talked for a long time; he was very persuasive about the seriousness of the situation, the need for the best possible information being available to government so that progress could be made towards a solution. He was sure I would want to do all I could to help, and my contacts as a journalist would make me very useful.

As he continued, he dropped into the conversation little bits of information about my own background - the street in Lisburn where my mother lived, the church she went to, small items that indicated he, or 'they', knew all about me. I felt alarmed, and by now I was so paranoid that I assumed these were threats. All I wanted to do was escape from the Europa and have some time to think. What would 'they' do if I simply said here and now, 'No thanks, not interested?' Was I already compromised? Would they twist my arm by suggesting they might make it known I had already been working for 'them' for several months, thus wrecking my journalistic career?

At which point my ever-polite Englishman suggested I think it over and give him a ring in a day or two. I agreed, and bolted from the Europa. I phoned him the next day and told him there was no way I could say yes; I could not go and talk to politicians today as a journalist, and then report back to him the next day. Sorry, but no thanks. To my surprise he said that was a pity, and if I changed my mind, I still had his phone number.

I spent the following weeks expecting all sorts of repercussions – a threatening phone call, a knock at my door, rumours about me. But nothing. I never heard from him again. Or not quite – the following December I received a card from the institute, wishing me a Happy Christmas and a Prosperous New Year, signed by him. I told no one but my wife about all this. It was years before I mentioned it to some close friends. For some months I searched my memory of the lunches I had had, but could find no recollection of having passed on any information that had not already appeared in print.

Then I began to wonder if my experience was unique; how many of my colleagues had similarly been approached, and how had they reacted? I never found out, but I could not help noticing how some of them spoke highly of the food in the restaurant at Bloom's Hotel. I cannot recall ever seeing Major McDowell there.

Thirteen

Press Gang

A newspaper reporter spends as much of his time in the company of journalists from other papers as he does with his own colleagues. The press tends to hunt as a pack, so *The Irish Times* was not the only new world into which I had to introduce myself. It could have been difficult; I don't think I knew personally a single journalist from any of the other papers when I started. They, on the other hand, knew each other very well; many had started together on provincial papers. The Dublin press corps at the end of the 1960s was a small one, dominated by journalists from the *Independent*, the *Press* and ourselves, plus the smaller Dublin office of *The Cork Examiner*. RTE was just beginning to make an impact.

I was an outsider, not just a Northerner, a Protestant to boot. But it made no difference, and I found myself warmly welcomed in the Dáil Gallery, at briefings, at press conferences, and wherever a marking might take me. Elder statesmen like Michael Mills, Arthur Noonan, Sean MacReamond, and even John Healy, were welcoming and helpful. I say 'even John Healy', for on top of John's brusque, and at times uncouth, manner, he was not looked on kindly by *Irish Times* regulars. They saw him as a personal favourite of Gageby, who was muscling in on the territory of the much loved Michael McInerney, for whom I was deputising when our paths crossed in the Dáil.

From 1969 onwards the prospect of Irish membership of the EEC meant that I became part of a group of four or five correspondents who *per force* became specialists in things European. At the start there were Frank Darcy of the *Independent*, Joe Carroll, freshly returned from Paris, of the *Press*, John (Stats) Feeney of RTE and myself. Shortly after that we were joined by Val Dorgan from *The Cork Examiner*, and Frank Darcy was replaced by Raymond (Congo) Smith. Later still, after Joe and John both went to Brussels to work for the European Commission, the odd-ball nature of the group was considerably enhanced by Julian de Kassel and Andy Shepherd.

We were a disparate group, thrown together, initially, by monthly trips to Brussels to cover the entry negotiations, and by even more frequent briefings and lunches with officials from Foreign Affairs. Some people, unaccountably, find EEC, now EU, matters tedious and boring. My experience, over a decade and a half of reporting Europe in the company of the stalwarts of the Dublin press corps, was of unfettered hilarity descending at times towards lunacy.

The tone was set on my first journalistic foray into the heart of the EEC in June 1970, when formal negotiations were opened, in Luxembourg, between the Ministers of the Six, and those of the four applicants, Denmark and Norway along with the UK and Ireland. Aer Lingus put on a special flight from Dublin to Luxembourg to carry out the Minister, Dr Paddy Hillery, and his officials, and half a dozen members of the press. During the flight the captain came back from the cockpit to greet his distinguished payload, and told the Minister that we were making history in more ways than one – this was the first time an Aer Lingus plane had flown into Luxembourg.

This item of news greatly impressed the Irish Ambassador to Belgium, who was also accredited to Luxembourg, and who was on board to ensure the safe arrival of his Minister. A diplomat of the old school, Gerry Woods was no blasé jet setter, and had already required several G&Ts to settle his nerves. Then the thought suddenly struck him that if no Aer Lingus plane had ever flown into Luxembourg, it meant this pilot had never been there; how then would he find the place, never mind land safely? The rest of the flight was spent assuring the Ambassador that these matters were best left to the professionals, and sedating him with more G&Ts.

The small group of reporters on that trip were under the pastoral care of Ed FitzGibbon, the Foreign Affairs diplomat who was press officer at the Embassy in Brussels. Ed was to become a friend and near constant companion over the next few years. A bearded Falstaffian figure, who was also an opera singer of standing, and bore some physical resemblance to the then rising star Pavarotti, he saw it as his duty on occasions such as that first trip to Luxembourg to introduce the press corps to the finer reaches of continental cuisine. In Luxembourg this meant the Café du Commerce in the Place du Commerce.

A memorable dinner there was the first chance for us journalists to come to know each other. In many ways I was the odd man out, but in fact I was outflanked in oddity by Raymond (Congo) Smith of the *Independent*. The others all knew him, or knew about him, but his appointment to cover the EEC negotiations was a surprise, and indeed was taken by one or two as something of an affront. He had achieved prominence, and his nickname, years earlier for his reporting of the Irish involvement in the UN peacekeeping mission in the Congo. He had also covered, and single-handedly disrupted world press coverage of Bobby Kennedy's funeral in Washington – by tripping over, and disconnecting the main power cable at Arlington Cemetery – but had been for some years the *Indo's* star reporter of Gaelic games. Just why he was now to cover the intricate political and economic complexities of EEC membership was not immediately clear.

He was a thin gangly individual, some years older than the rest of us with a shock of grey hair and an almost impenetrable, to me, Tipperary or Limerick accent. He talked non-stop, about great games he had seen, horse races, places and events across rural Ireland, all laced with outrageous stories involving himself which instantly reduced the teller and sometimes the audience to helpless laughter. As a result, the ordering of the meal was delayed, to the growing impatience of a very solid Luxembourgish waiter, who had stationed himself beside our table, tapping his foot as he gazed at the ceiling.

We were all ready to order except Ray. He had no French, so Ed FitzGibbon translated the menu for him. As he went through the long list, Raymond's confusion increased, along with a suspicion that his leg was being pulled. Then he came to *escargots*, 'What's dem, Ed?' 'Snails, Ray, very tasty.'

Raymond's eyebrows shot up. 'God FitzGibbon, you're a terrible man,' he declared and then turned to the waiter, demanding, in one breath, 'Creamot omatoandasteakwelldone.' Over the next decade Ray, in turns, drove us mad and gave us endless laughs.

Language remained a problem, not so much for him, as for those trying to understand him. During the entry negotiations in 1971, the question of a proposed EEC fisheries policy became a major issue. It came to a head very late one night during a negotiation at Ministerial level in Brussels. The talks dragged on into the night and early morning, with the journalists on the ground floor being fed infrequent morsels of information from the private dealings in the Council chamber.

As time passed, and deadlines expired, we Irish – with much later deadlines – were almost the only journalists left. Then the familiar summons – *Les journalistes sont invités* – led to a stampede to the lifts as 5 a.m. was striking. The immediate whisper as we filed into the Council chamber was that the EEC side had conceded, and agreed to shelve the proposed common fisheries policy. My Irish colleagues were elated, for fish had been a big issue at home. The French Foreign Minister, Maurice Schumann, then President of the Council of Ministers, filed in with Dr Hillery and other Ministers and Commissioners.

Before he could say a word, Ray was on his feet demanding to know, in his rich accent, 'Is it true, Mister Schumann, that fish is now a dead duck?' In our headphones we could hear a confused translator muttering to a colleague '*Qu'est-ce qu'il veut dire? Un canard mort?*'

Ray had a brief from Independent House to cater for the readers of the *Evening Herald,* and was ever on the lookout for what might appeal to the lower end of the market. As the *Herald* was an evening paper with very early deadlines, this search began at daybreak. One morning, before nine, Ray and I found ourselves on the steps of the Kirchberg building in Luxembourg waiting for a vital Council of Ministers meeting to begin. Sicco Mansholt, the President of the Commission, had the previous day threatened to walk out of the negotiation if the Council ignored his proposals.

As we stood chatting, a large car drew up at the foot of the steps, and Mansholt strode up towards us. Ray charged over; 'Is it true, Mr Mansholt, that you are walking out?' 'As you can see, I am walking in,' replied the imperturbable Mansholt as he swept past us. Ray was off like a shot, shouting back to me 'God, Dennis that's a great story for the *Herald.* Mansholt says he's walking in, not out.'

One particular issue in those early days was a thing called 'parallelism' – the principle that the EEC's negotiations on terms of membership with Ireland and the UK should proceed in parallel. The Government in Dublin was concerned that priority might be given to reaching a deal with London, leaving Ireland with something of a *fait accompli.* When the word first came up Ray informed us that he was not using it; the punter reading the *Herald* would not know what the hell he was talking about. (He had an engaging frankness about his story selection, and would announce to everyone within earshot what he was 'going on', as he started typing. He was not going on parallelism.)

When he found that I was keeping *The Irish Times* up to date on parallelism, it became a matter for much leg-pulling at my expense. After one round of negotiations, the press conference was totally dominated by parallelism, and as we were filing out of the room I heard Ray roaring after me 'God, Kennedy, you'll be massive in *The Irish Times* tomorrow.'

His specialist subject was horse racing, and he regaled us non-stop with tales of races, jockeys, trainers, bookies and betting coups. I knew nothing about racing and cared less, and while the others were more interested, none shared Ray's fanaticism on the subject, and we all took his stories with more than a pinch of salt. That was up until 1981. In June of that year we were all down in Killarney for a political seminar on the European Parliament. Ray informed us one morning that he was skipping the afternoon session as he wanted to watch the Derby from Epsom on TV.

Presentation to Dr Hillery on his appointment as European Commissioner, January 1973. From left: the author, Dr Hillery, Raymond Smith (*Irish Independent*), Val Dorgan (*Cork Examiner*) and Julien De Kassel (*Irish Press*). (Photo: Lensmen Photographic Archive.)

The sun was shining, the lakes sparkling and we all fancied a day out in the fresh air, so we said we would go with him, knowing the Derby would not take up too much of our time. All the way up to the Hotel Europe – Ray liked to watch his television in comfortable surroundings – he kept telling us about this tip he had had months earlier from some trainer down the country about a great young horse that was going to win the Derby. 'I put £50 on a twenty to one, and now you could hardly get a bet, he's down to evens or odds on,' he told us. This news confirmed our view that Ray had more than one slate loose. The horse's name meant nothing to us.

In the plush and almost deserted lounge of the Hotel Europe we ordered drinks and sat down at our ease. Not Ray; he paced around like a thoroughbred waiting for the off, and then they were off. We watched in open-mouthed amazement as Ray's tip took the lead and then raced almost out of sight of the rest of the field, while Ray galloped around the lounge roaring his support. We never forgot Shergar's name after that, and we paid a bit more attention to Ray's racing gossip.

He was also a bit of a philosopher; late at night, in Brussels or Strasbourg, after a good meal he would remove the glasses, rub his eyes, throw the head back and gaze down the considerable length of his great nose and pronounce on the human condition. 'Lads, there are two great things in life – sex and floury potatoes. And, you know, I think the floury potatoes has it.' He was a genuine one-off, and a great friend and comrade.

Val Dorgan, of the *Cork Examiner*, was also an expert on Gaelic games and all things sporting, and, like Raymond, a great companion on a trip. His moment of fame came on a visit to a still harshly divided Berlin in the late 1970s. Four of us had been invited to a UN conference in West Berlin, and my colleagues were anxious to cross the Wall and visit the East at the end of the seminar. As the only one who had previously crossed from West to East Berlin, I explained how we could do it and what was required. So, armed with our passports, we took the *S Bahn* towards *Friedrichstrasser* and crossed over the chilling vista of the Wall and the sterile death strip beyond it.

At *Friedrichstrasser*, which smelt strongly of Jeyes Fluid, we descended to the security checkpoint, myself in the lead, followed by Val. As I had explained, you pushed your passport under a green baize curtain at the little booth, and waited until it had been scrutinised by eyes unseen, and it remerged from under the green curtain. After the customary unnerving short delay, my passport reappeared, and I passed on, waiting beyond the security area for my colleagues.

Val had pushed his passport under the curtain, and was now awaiting its return. Several minutes passed, but no passport. Several more passed, and suddenly the *Cork Examiner* was being led away by two burly security police. My other colleagues came through with no bother, and we stood around waiting for Val. None of us was fluent enough in German to make headway with the transport officials, and the police just ignored our approaches.

After forty minutes an ashen-faced Val reappeared, and told us he had been held alone in a small room for half an hour or more, with no one coming near him. He had then been given his passport and waved through. He had no idea what it was all about. I had a look at his passport, and began to understand. In those days your passport had room for two photos, one of yourself and one of your spouse, in case you were travelling on a joint passport. Once stuck in, each photo was stamped across the edge to prove it was where it belonged.

Except in this case, there was no photo in the spot reserved for the holder, though the partial stamp showed there once had been. Instead, Val's likeness, with the remainder of the stamp on its top corner, was grinning out from the spot reserved for his spouse. The penny dropped as Val explained that when he had turned up at the start of the UN conference, he had been asked for the passport photo he had been told to bring with him to get accreditation. He had forgotten, but being a resourceful journalist, had ripped his picture from his passport, and used it instead. That morning, the conference being over, he had taken the picture off his badge, and hurriedly restored it to his passport, not noticing that he had stuck it in the wrong spot.

We presumed that the East German security police, ever alert for people trying to escape from East to West on false documents, had spent the forty minutes trying to understand why someone should try to get into East Germany on a transparently doctored passport.... and had then given up.

Other trips which we journalists specialising in European affairs enjoyed came courtesy of our own travel club; it was called the Association of European Journalists. Just before Ireland joined the EEC a couple of us were contacted by the Association secretary in Brussels, invited to a conference and put under gentle pressure to form a branch in Dublin. The AEJ was, at least until we joined, a serious, and sober body of senior journalists drawn from the original six member states of the EEC and the United Kingdom. Many of them had been through the Second World War, and had emerged from the French resistance, the Luxembourg army, Russian prison camps,

Italian internment camps and Lord knows where, determined to do what they could to unite Europe in peace, and banish war for ever.

They were remarkable people – almost all men – and it was both a privilege and an education to mix with them and share something of their dreadful experiences. We set up a branch in Dublin, with myself as chairman and soon discovered that whatever Dublin journalists lacked in earnest enthusiasm for the European ideal was more than made up for by their willingness to turn up for monthly lunches of the AEJ. We usually had a speaker – a Minister, a Commissioner, an Opposition Spokesman, the odd Taoiseach – which meant, of course, that attending journalists could claim the lunch on their expenses. For many years these were held in the convivial setting of the Elm Park Golf Club, and probably did more for the Europeanisation of Irish public opinion than all the referendum campaigns put together.

The highlight of the AEJ year was the annual conference, hosted in turn by the branches in the major cities of Europe. After sampling the delights of Lille, Mainz, Nice and Athens, we were caught off-balance at a meeting of the Comité Directeurs, and before we could stop him, Raymond Smith had volunteered Dublin for the next one. Somehow we managed to organise it, and up to 200 European journalists met for the formal session in Dublin Castle, opened by President Hillery, before embarking on a short tour to Limerick and Galway.

For me, as chairman and organiser, this was both a nightmare and a culturally enlightening experience. We had hired a train to take us from Heuston to Limerick; before we reached Limerick, the CIE men on board came to me to apologise that they had had to close the bar – it had been drunk dry. At Limerick we were decanted onto coaches which took us to Knappogue for a long medieval lunch. Then back on the coaches heading north to Galway, trying, in gathering winter gloom, to make up time so that we could reach the rendezvous point outside Galway, agreed with the Industrial Development Authority which we had persuaded to sponsor a dinner and overnight in Galway. We were to tour the Galway Industrial estate before booking into the Great Southern for dinner.

All was well until we reached Gort. Then nature intervened, and we had to obey its call and stop. Assorted Europeans piled out of the three or four coaches as I shouted that they had just ten minutes. They disappeared into the several pubs around the square. Ten minutes later I sat alone in the first coach; not even the drivers had come back.

After another ten minutes I went into the nearest pub, to find that a music session was in full swing, and no one had any intention of leaving. I told them the buses would be pulling out in fifteen minutes, with or without them, which message I repeated in the other pubs. Fifteen minutes passed, and I was still alone. Then the drivers straggled back. I looked at my watch, and decided that we would be leaving in exactly ten minutes, with or without the cream of European journalism. I meant it.

Just before the deadline, the trickle back began, and was in full, if rather unsteady flood when I told the drivers to start up. I was furious, and extremely worried about the IDA. That body was run by deadly serious young men who had agreed to sponsor us only after we had supplied a list of the delegates to our conference, and had they been assured that many of them were very important writers on finance and business in their respective countries. We were going to be at least an hour late, and it was now dark and raining.

I was in the first coach, and when we reached the rendezvous point, there was no one there. The second coach was just pulling in when the IDA men emerged from the darkness. I apologised abjectly, and they said not a bother; when we had not turned up they had just adjourned to the pub. One of them got into each coach and we set off. In ours the IDA man took the tour-guide's microphone briefly welcomed us to Galway, and then announced he was going to sing a song. And he did, a flawless rendition of 'I'm my own Grandpaw'. The dinner was a riotous success, thoroughly enjoyed by everyone, except the tight-lipped senior executive from the IDA who delivered his deadly serious talk in something less than hushed silence, and me, whose nerves were still in overdrive.

Lying in bed in the Great Southern that night I had a moment of great truth; I realised, I had been taking myself, and life, too seriously. What would have happened if I had indeed driven off from Gort with empty coaches? The journalists would have had a whale of a time in the pubs, would somehow have found their way to Galway, or to beds somewhere else. The IDA men would have finished the evening in the pub outside Galway and gone home, wondering idly what had become of that coach party that was supposed to turn up.

No one would have died, except perhaps the senior IDA man, from apoplexy, and myself, from hypertension. And the journalists would have returned, eventually, to the four corners of Europe swearing that that was the best conference ever – which they did anyway. I was learning that while things in this part of Ireland may be desperate, they are never too serious.

Fourteen

Budget Travel

My job in the *Irish Times* involved not just trips to many parts of the EEC, but to further and more exotic locations, and often on my own rather than as a member of the pack. The paper was by no means wealthy, but Gageby saw such journalism as an important part of the improvements he was constantly making to it. He never made any issue over expenses, though we were not encouraged to throw money around.

One day in November 1969 I was at my desk when he came out of his office and asked me could I get to South Africa as soon as possible and write about apartheid. A Springbok rugby tour was about to begin, including a match in Dublin against Ireland, and a campaign against it was gathering weight. 'Get there and stay for two or three weeks, or until the money runs out. I can manage £500, so see how far it goes.'

I rang the South African Embassy in London and asked about a visa, telling them I was a journalist. The strong accent on the other end asked me if I was white. I had never been asked that before, and was a bit nonplussed. I replied that as it was November I was more a shade of slatey grey. He was unamused, but said as I had an Irish passport I did not need a visa.

Two days later I was on a flight from London to Johannesburg, with £500 in my pocket, and two lists of people I might contact. One list was in my head; it had been given to me by Kadar Asmal, then a lecturer in Trinity and head of the Irish Anti-Apartheid Movement. As it consisted of various

ANC members and supporters, Kadar had insisted I memorise it and then destroy it. The other, for which no such fate had been demanded, had come from my university friend and rugby player, Davy Hewitt, who had toured South Africa with the Lions and made many friends.

I had had no time to make hotel arrangements, so when, on landing at Johannesburg's Jan Smutts' International Airport, I was asked by Emigration Control where I was staying, I said I had no idea. 'We must have an address for you in South Africa, so tell me which hotel you are staying in.' 'Which would you recommend?' I asked. 'The Victoria is good. I will put that down.'

I found the Victoria, booked in and slept for hours. I awoke to the strains of a choir singing 'Onward Christian Soldiers' which added to my disori-entation. (It was Sunday, and there was an Anglican church right across the street from my hotel window.) I then noticed how much the room was costing, and with my £500 limit in mind, promptly paid my bill and left, finding a much cheaper small hotel, owned by an affable Greek.

Two or three mornings later I was wakened shortly after six by the phone in my room. A strong South African accent asked if that was Mr Kennedy. I said it was. 'Emigration at Jan Smutts International' the voice said 'We thought you were staying at the Victoria.' 'Far too expensive for me.' 'So you are now at the Monte Carlo?' I said I was and he said thank you and hung up.

A weekly ticket on the buses, a diet consisting largely of a South African speciality – banana and cheese sandwiches – and the low cost of living, saw the £500 displaying considerable stamina. I was able to take a train down to Durban, then a flight to Capetown, and then a magic train journey all the way back to Johannesburg, via the Karoo, Kimberly, Mafeking and other chapters from British history. (In deference to my budget, this was the Brown Train, not the fabled Blue.)

My Greek host had allowed me to leave my luggage in my room at the Monte Carlo, free of charge as things were very slack. Next morning, the phone again awoke me shortly after six. It was my friend from Emigration, Jan Smutts International. 'Is that you Mr Kennedy? We hear you have been to Durban?' 'Yes, and what's more, I've been to Capetown.' 'Have you indeed? But now you are back in Johannesburg at the Monte Carlo?' I assured him I was, and he wished me good bye.

At the end of just over four weeks in South Africa, I had spent the £500 and run out of clean socks and shirts, and was on my way home. Waiting in the lobby for a taxi – a final extravagance – I was enjoying a chat with my Greek host. 'Tell me, Mr Kennedy, are you a journalist or something?' I admitted to the former and he smiled. 'I thought you must be. Certain people were very interested in you. Was everything OK with your luggage when you came back?'

My room, it transpired, had been searched in my absence. I was glad I had taken Kadar's advice and destroyed the list of ANC contacts. I often wonder what the Security Police made of my other list – consisting almost entirely of Afrikaner rugby types, and Davy Hewitt's Plymouth Brethren co-religionists. I felt rather pleased that I had managed to break the rules, with impunity, on at least two occasions during my stay.

Early in my visit I made contact with *Drum*, the radical magazine produced in Johannesburg mainly by black staff. They asked me if I wanted to go to Soweto, which was strictly off-limits for visiting white journalists. They would be happy to smuggle me in that evening when they were going home, so I found myself lying cramped on the floor of a VW beetle, under the feet of the back-seat passengers. We had no problems, and I spent several hours in the township before leaving in the style in which I had entered.

Right at the start of my visit I had gone to see the Bantu courts in action, or I had tried to. These were the courts busily despatching large numbers of blacks deemed to be living illegally in white areas, in breach of the infamous Pass Laws. The courts were held in a clutch of one-story wooden buildings, a bus-ride from the city centre in a run-down area close to the main railway marshalling yards.

On a blistering hot morning I presented myself at the police post at the entrance to the complex and said I wanted to sit in on one of the courts. The policeman said I would have to have the permission of the magistrate holding the court, which seemed odd. I was marched to another building and ushered into the magistrate's room. He was all affability, greeted me warmly, asked me about Ireland, and why I wanted to come into his court. I told him I was writing about apartheid, and this seemed to be the sharp end of the system.

He said I was most welcome, and he was sure once I had seen for myself I would understand apartheid and why it was the best way forward for all races in South Africa. He would be very happy to have me in his court, but not today. I asked why. Because I was not properly dressed. I was wearing a sparkling clean white shirt and freshly pressed trousers, but I did not have a jacket and I did not have a tie. The dignity of the court had to be respected. I said I would return the next day with those defects remedied, and he said he would be pleased to welcome me.

So I did, and he invited me to sit beside him on the bench, an invitation which I declined. He said I could sit at the back, and we walked over to another low shed-like building, passing on the way a series of wire cages crowded with black men and women. I took my seat on a wooden bench at the back of the small empty room, while my host moved up to the desk on a raised platform at the front. It was sweltering hot; the windows along one side were open, but they faced onto railway sidings, and the room was periodically filled with the acrid smoke from steam engines shunting up and down.

Proceedings began when a side door close to the platform opened and the prisoners were marched in rapid succession from the wire cages. A couple of minutes sufficed to deal with each one, who was then marched out another door, and straight on to a lorry parked outside. I later learned that the lorries drove the prisoners straight to their designated homeland, and dumped them with some timber and sheets of corrugated iron, and left them to make their own homes – often in areas they had never known, and where, sometimes, they did not speak the local language. But it was all legal, done according to the book, with due respect for the law, in front of a properly dressed audience.

Outside the courts I waited in the heat for a bus back to my hotel. One came and I was about to board it when I noticed the large notice on the front 'Swartz. Niet blanks'. Two more came, similarly labelled for Blacks only, and after forty minutes I gave up and found a taxi. My magistrate friend would have said that showed how fair apartheid was, for the best for all races.

It was my visit to the Bantu courts that led indirectly to my second flouting of the laws of the land. I was in Durban, interviewing an Indian family active in political protest. As I was about to leave, an unexpected visitor arrived; he was a priest, a young Corkman, and he was bringing a package for the family from their son who was a doctor in KwaZulu, where the priest was stationed. He heard I had been to the Bantu courts and he asked me if I wanted to see what happened to the people who passed through them. He was driving back that night to the small town where he was curate, and I could go with him, and he could take me down into the Zulu homelands to see for myself.

As we drove through the night he said it would be better if I slipped into the parochial house without anyone seeing me, and stayed in my room until he came for me in the morning. He did not want his Parish Priest to know about me, and he did not want anyone in the small town telling the magistrate a white visitor had arrived and was staying with the priests. (The town was high on the veldt, surrounded by deep valleys which were designated Zulu homelands.)

In the morning he arrived at my room clutching a clerical collar. It would be better, if I did not mind, if I wore it, because no one would pass any remark on another priest accompanying him down into the settlement areas. As a white visitor I could go there only with the written authority of the magistrate, and there was no way a journalist would get that. So for the next two days I was Umfundezi Kennedy, seeing at first hand the appalling conditions suffered by those deported from white areas, and maintaining what I felt was an air of priestly concern.

By the time I left I had written and airmailed a dozen articles on apartheid — airmailed because my visit would probably have been cut short by expulsion had the articles appeared while I was still there. I sent a telegram to Gageby saying I had spent all the money and was coming home. I received a quick reply. 'Great stuff. Stay on if you like. I'll find some more money.'

But I had had enough of cheese and banana sandwiches, of scorching sunshine, and of apartheid. When I arrived back in the office, Gageby said 'Great stuff. Take a week off to recover.' So I had seven December days in Glencullen to cool off.

Fifteen

Something She Ate

Having two young children when we arrived in Glencullen, plus a new baby in 1974, certainly helped embed us in village life. For most of a decade we needed babysitters, and one of the great advantages of living in Glencullen was the plentiful supply of people ready to serve as such, even at the shortest notice. Nor was there any question of driving them home after a late night. So we were soon on very friendly terms with a small but widening circle, and through them we learned more and more about the rest of the village.

As our children began to grow up, they made particular friends and they were all in and out of our house and theirs, so through the uninhibited confidences of children we had more insights into Glencullen. 'What's the height of ignorance?' a neighbour's young lad demanded of us one spring day. We expressed our own ignorance on that one. 'A six foot Kerryman,' he replied bursting into laughter, then adding that the Master at Glencullen school was both six foot tall and from Kerry.

Another day another young fellow was sitting in our kitchen going over the latest news. Young X, he told us, was pregnant. We were a bit surprised that he even knew what that meant, but also at the news itself, for young X was a singularly unattractive and fiercesome girl who worked in a local stables, took no care of herself at all and invariably exuded a rich aroma of horse dung. Forgetting our informant was still there listening to us, we wondered aloud how on earth the pregnancy could have come about. An explanation was at hand, 'My Da says it must have been something she ate,' came the helpful interjection from the other side of the kitchen.

The same source solved for us the mystery of Mr Manning's van. The Mannings were an elderly couple who lived in one half of what had been the old barracks – a long low cottage right on the roadside. Mr Manning's small red van, also elderly, was usually parked on the road, alongside the cottage and close up to it. I had noticed when out walking at night that a heavy black cable seemed to be attached to the underside of the van, and ran through a hole in the frame of the window in the front wall of the cottage. I was intrigued by the cable, and wondered if Mr Manning had perfected some means of powering the van by mains electricity, or at least of starting it that way on icy mornings. 'No way,' said my youthful informant, 'Dat's his burglar alarm. Dat wire's tied to the end of the scratcher, so if anybody tries to nick the van, they'll give the bed a yank and wake him up.'

On one occasion we found ourselves short of a babysitter. All our regulars were doing something else, and we were at a loss. 'Sure, Ena Cotter will do it for you,' said a neighbour, 'I'll ask her for you if you like.' We were a bit doubtful, for our only close encounter with Ena, who had just recently come back to live in Glencullen, had been one Sunday afternoon while we were out walking down near Glencullen Bridge and our dog became involved in a murderous encounter with another dog. As I tried to haul our fellow to safety, Ena, who was also out walking, intervened. The voice and the vocabulary soon cowed the combatants into submission. I had then not yet seen her in action as the champion of the 44B travelling public against the shortcomings of CIE and its buses.

We were desperate, so we said yes, and Ena became a favourite with all our children, second only to our next door neighbour, Betty Mulvey. Like Betty, Ena was soon our friend too, and a source of great amusement over the years. She contributed generally to our children's education and to their vocabulary in particular.

Despite the fact that she and her husband were among the most devoted couples we had ever known, and he the most amiable and useful of men, she invariably referred to him in conversation as 'That bugger John Cotter,' and attributed all manner of shortcomings to him. The name cropped up in our children's conversation, and we realised that our sons were referring to a key item of their male equipment as their 'Johnny Cotter', a piece of terminology picked up when Ena had been supervising bath-time.

Another bath-time gem was her admonition on the dangers of fiddling with one's belly-button. 'Look you,' she warned one night, as we were told later, 'I'd be careful with that. I knew a young fella once was fiddling with that, and he twisted it and his arse fell off.'

Ena's favourite word was one of her own; 'Damnedable' was the biting epithet applied to everything from bad weather to CIE.

In one vital respect our children did not and could not integrate fully into Glencullen; not being Catholic, they did not walk the half mile to the village school, but instead were driven the three miles down the hill to Kilternan National School No2, as the Church of Ireland primary school was officially labelled. We did not particularly like this arrangement, as we were not Church of Ireland, had little connection with Kilternan, and were faced with the daily chore of delivering and collecting our children.

But it was not really our choice. I would have much preferred to send my children to a school with no religious affiliation, but living in what was, essentially, a confessional state, that option was not available, so we had to choose between a Catholic school and a Protestant one, and we chose Protestant.

Going to different schools had little if any impact on the close friendships our children had already begun to make, but there were one or two surprises. When the school yard at Glencullen was transformed into a tarmac tennis court, and the village children encouraged to use it, and learn to play, our two older ones were keen to join in. They already had tennis rackets, and knew many of the children, but when they turned up one day they were told that, as they were not pupils at the school, they could not play. And when a local man offered to give guitar lessons after school to anyone who wanted them, our older son was mad keen to go, only to be told he could not – he was not a pupil at the school. (Some time after that, when the tennis court at Kilternan Parish Church was repaired and efforts made to start a club, Katherine and I were eager players. But when a Catholic couple with whom we were friendly approached us about playing, it was discreetly intimated to us that they should not be encouraged.)

All three of our children did time at Kilternan No 2. When the first one started there in 1971 the enrolment was down to about twenty, and the school was under threat of closure. Classes were still held in the nineteenth-century single story one-room schoolhouse behind the church, under the firm hand of Miss Sloan, a teacher cut from the same cloth as the building, and one assistant. A campaign was beginning to save the school, so our delivery of one new pupil, and the promise of another in a year, meant we were very welcome.

Kilternan and the surrounding area was becoming a fashionable retreat, and the school numbers increased, so much so that it was decided to put up an additional modern, timber, two-room building behind the old school, allowing separate classes to be held and an additional teacher employed. All this meant fund-raising, and voluntary labour, as we did the building work ourselves. So between hammering and sawing, parents' meetings, travelling suppers and sales of work, we found ourselves part of, or at least on the edge of, a small world that was neither Glencullen nor *The Irish Times*. It was our first real contact with Southern Protestant society.

The travelling supper was, to us, a new method of fund-raising. It consisted of a four course meal, each course, and venue, provided by a different family. So we met for *hors d'oeuvres* in one house, moved on to the main course in another, had dessert in a third, and ended up for coffee in a fourth. As an element of competition inevitably entered into the exercise, we were guaranteed excellent fare as well as a crash course in meeting other parents and parish members.

The parish was made up of well-to-do families who had been established in Kilternan for generations – big farmers, business people – plus newcomers to the area who were mostly professional, and mostly rich. A bit to our surprise we found that there was a vital element that was working class, or just beginning to migrate socially upwards. Not all Southern Protestants had money, or had been educated at Trinity, or indeed at any university or secondary school.

We were invited to join Kilternan parish, and went a few times to Sunday service in the attractive little church. One new friend, who also had children at the school, was very keen for us to join, and kept stressing the rather odd incentive that we would qualify for a grave in the churchyard; 'A lovely place to be buried,' he enthused. We were not into such long-term planning, and anyway, non-conformist that I was, I had little taste for the formalism and ritual of the Church of Ireland.

Even so, we became sort of non-subscribing members, through the school, and then through the tennis. The high-light of the school year was the annual outing to Brittas Bay; it had been going for years before we became involved and was traditional in every respect. An ancient privately-owned double-decker bus was hired, always the same one, to carry the children, and, accompanied by a flotilla of cars, it would trundle down into Wicklow and the open beaches and rolling sand hills of Brittas.

A picnic, races on the sand, races in the water, a sandcastle competition, were all only temporary interruptions to lolling on the beach and gossiping, or, if the weather was not great, to huddling under blankets to keep warm. The weather was one of two uncertain factors, the other was the ageing bus and whether it would ever make it to Brittas, or having done so, would ever make it home again.

We came to know and like the Kilternan people, and to understand them a little better. The threatened closure of the school had made them sharply aware of what a vulnerable minority they were. The parish had lost families through mixed marriages, and it was clear that there was a persistent fear that their young people would find romance with Catholic partners and, inevitably, abandon the Church of Ireland. That, I am sure, was behind the reluctance to welcome Catholics into the tennis club.

None of this was discussed openly, nor was politics. When the Northern Troubles were at their worst, only one or two of the younger men ever raised the issue with me, even though I was a journalist, a Northerner and a frequent visitor to the North. For the most part it was heads down.

Not finding the prospect of a grave in Kilternan church yard sufficient to entice me into the arms of Anglicanism, I still had to find somewhere to worship. Just as our earlier house-hunting had given me a greatly improved knowledge of the geography of Dublin, now my spiritual quest broadened my appreciation of church architecture as I sampled morning worship in Church of Ireland, Presbyterian and Methodist churches from Dundrum to Dún Laoghaire from Blackrock to Bray and from Rathgar to Ranelagh. On one occasion I found myself sitting in a small room on Northumberland Road peering at twin prints of William of Orange and Queen Mary and listening to a Baptist pastor. (The prints belonged, not to the Baptists, but to the Orange Lodge which owned the building.)

Almost by accident I discovered that a new Methodist congregation had been established in Dundrum, and was meeting in the hall of Taney Parish church. I went along and rather liked the informality of meeting in a hall, not a church, music supplied by a portable harmonium, of having coffee afterwards, and of finding a minister who believed that ten minutes was on the long side for a sermon. He had also, like me, been a hockey player, but in Cork, not Belfast. So I joined, and dragged my children along with me, and my wife occasionally. The church was officially Methodist, but the new congregation had brought together a core of Methodists and a mixture of Anglicans, Presbyterians, Plymouth Brethren and, it was rumoured, wandering Catholics. So on Sunday mornings I now had a fourth world to explore and observe – it was not Glencullen, not Kilternan, not *The Irish Times.*

Whether it was a result of the Methodist rule of rotating ministers every so many years, or not, this church showed much greater awareness of the Northern Troubles than had the Church of Ireland. Prayers were offered every week for peace in the North, in stark contrast to the Presbyterian Church I sometimes attended on visits home to Lisburn. There I was astounded one New Year at the height of the violence to sit through service and sermon dedicated to reviewing the past year and anticipating the one to come, and not hear a single reference to the mayhem or the political situation. Perhaps they came to church to get away from it.

Assiduous praying for Northern Ireland by the Dundrum Methodists did not mean they really understood the problem. The more I observed them, got to know the Kilternan Church of Ireland people, and still had ample opportunity to mix with Northern Protestants on my frequent visits North, the more I came to believe that the remarkable continued unity of the Protestant churches, post-partition, was based on mutual *mis*understanding North and South.

The Northerners were convinced that their Southern brethren were really Unionist at heart, but did not dare give any public indication of this, that they understood and shared the Unionist case, but could not actually say so. The Southerners, on the other hand, were inclined to the view that their Northern co-religionists were, at best, off their heads, and, at worst, raving bigots, but were much too polite to say so, or too aware that they belonged to churches that were dominated numerically by Northerners, and dependent financially on the Northern strength. Both sides were, to a degree, mistaken in these assumptions, but they served nicely to hold the churches together.

The Methodist rotation system meant that a considerable number of Ministers based in Dublin churches at any one time were Northerners. I was intrigued to find how easily, in practice, most of them fitted into the different environment – happily organising joint ventures with the parish priest, welcoming couples of mixed marriages, and not turning a hair when children of these marriages would turn up for morning service in their full first communion Catholic finery before proceeding to mass, or having already been.

But their sermons tended to confirm my theory of helpful mutual mis-understanding. One November, our morning service at Dundrum was taken by a long-serving Northerner who had for several years been sta-tioned in Dublin. It was close to Armistice Day, and, quite correctly, he spoke about the horrors of war and the sacrifices it entailed. But his main illustration was based on the heroic story of an RAF pilot and his part in the fire-bombing of Hamburg in the Second World War. Chatting over coffee after the service I asked him if, when telling that particular story, he had remembered that Ireland had been neutral in that particular war, and that not a few Irish people might argue that fire-bombing of German civilians was a war crime.

For good measure I added that his address to the children, which had been a story about two young girls, one born in poverty and the other a princess, had portrayed being a princess as the most desirable and wonder-ful status a young orphan might aspire to. Had he not remembered that we were in a republic, and that, by definition, we regarded princesses and other royalty as exploiters of the poor and leeches on society?

I was not being serious, just testing my theory. But he looked at me blankly, and moved away.

Sixteen

Diplomats Abroad

In December 1976, when Leonid Brezhnev was still ruling the Soviet Union, and the Cold War was going through a renewed chill, a belated thaw in relations between Dublin and Moscow meant I visited Russia for the first time.

I was accompanying Garret FitzGerald, then Ireland's Foreign Minister, who was going to Moscow on an official visit to sign a Cooperation Agreement between Ireland and the USSR. The first four days were spent in an icy-cold Moscow, culminating in the signing ceremony with Foreign Minister Gromyko and President Podgorny in the Kremlin. A neat irony was the fact that Gromyko had been the Soviet Union representative on the UN Security Council in 1946 who had vetoed Ireland's admission to the United Nations, on the grounds of her neutrality, and alleged Nazi sympathies, in the Second World War.

The Soviet authorities did not like foreign journalists wandering around on their own, so we – myself and three colleagues – were treated as part of the official party. We were picked up at our hotel and whisked in style in a large black Zil limousine across Red Square and through the gates of the Kremlin.

Later, we were transported to the Bolshoi Theatre, where, as part of the official visit, Garret and Joan FitzGerald were guests of honour at a gala performance. The ballet performed was based on Shakespeare's 'Much Ado about Nothing', which could have been a subtle comment from our hosts on the first official visit of an Irish Foreign Minister to the Soviet Union, had the Kremlin been given to subtlety.

The following morning the visit was scheduled to move on to Tbilisi, in Georgia. An official plane was provided and we were collected and delivered to the airport. As we boarded our private airliner, we were surprised to find that the ten or eleven that made up the entire Irish party were not the only ones there. We were joined by about a dozen Russians, most of whom we recognised as officials or party minders we had encountered over the previous three days, some now having with them their wives or girlfriends.

The mood was festive; brandy was served as we taxied out to the runway. Then, with the plane roaring into take off, the foreign-ministry official who was acting as our host, stood with his back braced against the bulkhead at the front of the plane, and proposed a toast. The message was clear – rules did not apply to important people.

The following days in Tbilisi were spent mainly in drinking more toasts, and seeing some of the sites of that intriguing city, sampling the thermal baths once patronised by Tolstoy.

After Tbilisi we were to fly back up north to Leningrad (it was still Leningrad). Our private plane was awaiting us, and this time we found our numbers swelled still further, as a batch of the Georgian toast-drinkers, plus wives and girlfriends, now joined us. So we arrived in Leningrad as a party of almost thirty. Leningrad in December was frighteningly cold. The Neva was frozen over, and the city looked magnificent. We had a private visit to the Winter Palace and the Hermitage – the public excluded to facilitate us. On our final night we were taken to see the Kirov perform at the Mariinskiy theatre. Garret and his wife Joan were installed in the Royal Box – still draped in Romanov blue – while the rest of us had prime seats outside it in the dress circle.

We were due to travel back to Moscow that night by train, on the midnight express. After the ballet a fleet of cars took us – Irish, Muscovites, Georgians, and of course, our new comrades from Leningrad – through the night into the forests outside the city to a government *dacha*. There we were entertained to a dinner, and invited to toast the health of Comrade Brezhnev, who that day was celebrating his seventieth birthday.

After dinner an unnerving race from the *dacha* to the station over icy roads saw us decanted onto the train. A special coach had been attached to it to carry the distinguished guests, though we journalists found ourselves

Winter in Leningrad, 1976. From left, Mike Burns (RTE), Russian interpreter, Sean
Cantwell (*Irish Independent*) and Michael Mills (*Irish Press*), author.

accommodated more modestly. But we were soon invited to join our bet-
ters. The special coach must have survived from Tsarist times. It contained
what looked like a large dining room, with an enormous polished mahogany table in the centre. It was loaded with impressive quantities of vodka,
brandy and Georgian wine. All around were our friends from Moscow and
Tbilisi, plus fresh reinforcements from Leningrad.

The next couple of hours constituted one of the most surreal experiences
of my journalistic career. As the assorted Russians and Georgians got drun-
ker and merrier, with their guests feeling obliged to join in, the toasts gave
way to singing, and even to dancing as portly apparatchiks waltzed with
each other. All this as we roared through the Russian night, with occasional
glimpses of birch forests deep in snow, lit up by the lights of the passing
train. I have often wondered since, did some of those apparatchiks realise,
far more clearly than we did, that the system was doomed, and that they had
better make the best of it while they could.

In January 1978, President Hillery went on a state visit to India. This was a jamboree to put the Soviet trip in the shade. Like that venture, the strictly official part lasted no more than a few days, taking in India's Republic Day celebration in Delhi and a dinner at Rastrapati Bhavan. At the dinner we solemnly drank toasts to India in rose water, as Delhi at that time, with the austere Moraji Desai as Prime Minister, was resolutely dry, as were many other parts of India.

The ceremony attending all such functions was very impressive. The Indians had learned to master pomp and ceremony at the hands of their colonial masters, and their military today could probably teach the Household Cavalry how to brush up its routines. I was a bemused spectator to much of this, listening to speeches in English from both sides celebrating their common experience of winning freedom from imperial Anglophone domination, and expressing mutual pride in the reassertion of their own cultures. When the band struck up *Tipperary* it seemed a nice touch, but I almost fell off my seat when, at one government reception, the military band launched into *Derry's Walls*. Equilibrium of a sort was recovered when I realised that it was *God Bless the Prince of Wales* they were playing, the tune of which, at least to my unmusical ear, is exactly the same. Under that title, it is, as is *Tipperary,* part of the standard repertoire of military music and ceremonial, originally British, but now almost universal.

We came across another real link between Ireland and India, which had not been mentioned in any speeches, when we visited Madras. There we met some Irish nuns who were teachers at a school mainly attended by children of mixed race. The most common surnames in the school, they told us, were O'Sullivan, Mulligan and Murphy.

Madras was part of a magical itinerary over two more weeks during which the Presidential caravan trekked, mainly by air, across vast swathes of the sub-continent, from Chandigarh in the Punjab, down to Agra, Bangalore, Madras, Madurai, Kerala, taking in Fatehpur Sikri, the Shore Temples at Mahabalipuram, the Caves at Ajanta and the Caves at Ellora, before ending up for a rest in Goa, and thence to Bombay via Aurangabad and a final visit to the Caves of Elephanta.

Being a Presidential outing, the accompanying party was much larger than that which had gone to Moscow. Mrs Hillery, disrespectfully referred to as Queen Maeve by the lower ranks of Foreign Affairs, accompanied the President as did his Aide de Camp. The Foreign Minister Michael

Callaghan of India: Leybourne Callaghan, Honorary Consul of Ireland at the Gateway to India, Bombay, January 1978.

O'Kennedy and his wife Breda were in attendance, as were assorted officials, and some wives, from Foreign Affairs. The press corps was swelled by the inclusion of an RTE camera crew. In all it took two elderly planes, put at our disposal by the Indian air force, to transport us around. Unlike Russia, there was no steady accretion of Indian free-loaders. We had a liaison officer of sorts, and, very exotic, a yogi put at the personal service of President Hillery, whose devotion to the practice of yoga had been telegraphed ahead by observant Indian diplomats in Dublin.

The yogi, Dr Chatrasall Singh, of the Central Research Institute for Yoga and the Ministry of Health and Social Welfare, according to his card which I still have, thought the opportunity of a lifetime had arrived; we were convinced he fully believed he would be joining the permanent establishment at *Áras an Uachtaráin*. He was sensitive about his status on the trip, and was anxious always to be on the first plane with the President, not consigned to the second with more junior officials, the press and the baggage.

He and Dr Hillery seemed to get on fine at the yoga. At one stop Mrs Hillery was asked in the hotel lobby if she had seen the President, as he was running late for something or other. She was heard to reply that the last time she had seen him he was standing on his head in his room with that bloody fakir, or words to that effect.

The yogi sensed that we of the press did not altogether take him too seriously. But he had us at his mercy in, I think it was Aurangabad, when, not for the first time, the planes were experiencing their own version of Delhi Belly. We had all arrived out at the small airport late on a beautiful afternoon. There was a delay. Then we learned that one plane was out of action, and that the other would fly ahead to Bombay, taking with it the Presidential party and its baggage. Dr Singh, surplus to requirements, had to make way for the baggage.

That left him with us journalists at the airport, as the sun started to go down, waiting against the half promise that a replacement plane would come for us. The airport staff began to wander off home, as no more flights were due in or out; we wandered out onto the runway, and before we knew it, the yogi had us sitting in a circle on the tarmac, taking in deep breaths to a count of ten and exhaling profoundly. I think he was deeply disappointed when we were shepherded off the runway to make way for the incoming replacement plane.

Few, if any, of the Irish party shared Dr Hillery's asceticism, certainly not as regards alcohol, but their needs were amply catered for in Mr Desai's alcohol-free India by the Department of Foreign Affairs. Several large, sinister-looking tin trunks, normally used to convey sensitive documents, accompanied the caravan, carefully loaded on and off flights. Packed with bottles of Powers, Jameson, allied spirits and fine wines they were opened in the privacy of hotel rooms.

In Bombay the entire party was taken under the sheltering wing of Ireland's Honorary Consul in Bombay, Leybourne Callaghan, the epitome of an Old India Hand, self-styled Callaghan of India, captain of the Indian Rugby XV, and long-serving executive of a large multi-national drugs firm in Bombay. His personal establishment included a Mercedes and a jeep bearing Church of Ireland plates, and a small army of retainers the epaulettes of whose uniforms were similarly decorated. Despite the Church of Ireland badge his religious connections were Methodist rather than Church of Ireland, and I already knew something of him through his brother the Revd Sydney Callaghan, sometime President of the Methodist Church in Ireland.

His mission in life seemed to be to prove that he could make things work efficiently in a country where many hundreds of millions were dedicated to ensuring that they did not. He did this by much roaring and shouting at his servants, feigned physical assaults, and a ritual of sending them fleeing for their lives round the courtyard of his building as he careered in at the wheel of his jeep – and also, I was told, by paying them considerably over the odds.

A Presidential visit, with several grand functions in Bombay, was a challenge he relished. A formal dinner was being given by the President in the Taj Mahal hotel for the cream of Irish expatriates. Nuns and Christian Brothers materialised from all parts, along with aid workers, captains of industry and others. At around five in the afternoon, an hour before the President was due to welcome his guests at a pre-dinner reception, a crisis arose. The President's dress suit had gone awol. Mrs Hillery had given it to a hotel flunky that morning to have it cleaned and pressed, and now it could not be found. It was lost.

Honorary Consul Callaghan set aside his gin and tonic in the hotel bar and took charge. He interrogated Mrs Hillery. Had she obtained a deposit or a signature from the flunkey when she had handed over the suit? She had not.

'Good God Ma'am, you should have had his balls for a deposit,' he exploded and strode off to wreak havoc, leaving a blushing Mrs Hillery not sure whether to be outraged or laugh. Whatever uproar Callaghan of India created in the bowels of the Taj Mahal hotel, the President duly appeared to welcome his guests in his dress suit, pristine and pressed.

Seventeen

Politicians

Three individuals dominated Irish politics during my days with *The Irish Times*: Jack Lynch, Garret FitzGerald and Charlie Haughey. I got to know all three of them, the first two more than the third.

In October 1968, a month or so after joining the paper, I was sent to cover a Fianna Fáil meeting in Dún Laoghaire on the referendum to abolish Proportional Representation. Jack Lynch, the Taoiseach, was the speaker. It was the first time I had seen him. I remember he spoke in a quiet concerned manner, and had very sad eyes. The civil rights agitation in the North, and the baton charge in Duke Street in Derry, were of more public interest than the referendum, so he concentrated on them. He was, he said, very concerned about the situation. When he had been persuaded to enter politics years earlier, he said, his main reason for doing so was concern for the North of Ireland.

Less than two years later, he invited me to join him at his table at a dinner in New York which he was giving for the Irish delegation to the 1970 celebrations of the United Nation's twenty-fifth anniversary. Our paths had crossed at one or two functions before that, but I had never had a conversation with him. By 1970 the unrest in Northern Ireland was much worse. As we sat down he said he wanted to talk to me about the North. 'Frankly', he said, 'I know very little about it. I really never gave it a thought until it all broke out.'

I couldn't resist reminding him of what he had said two years earlier that night in Dún Laoghaire. 'Ah, sure, never mind that. That's what every

Fianna Fáil politician has to say,' he replied with a smile, disarming me completely. We had a long conversation that night, and though thereafter I frequently disagreed with his politics, and criticised them in print, I also felt we remained friends.

I first met Charlie Haughey on the day in 1969 when, as Minister for Finance, he revealed the designs for the new decimal currency to be introduced in 1971. I was sent up to cover the press conference in Government Buildings in Merrion Street – my first time in that building. There were two or three other journalists waiting inside the entrance, to be called up to the Minister's office. About ten minutes later we were summoned up, and shown into the private office, where we waited another five minutes for the arrival of the Minister. (This was a pattern invariably repeated whenever Mr Haughey was involved.)

The young Charlie breezed in, flung himself into his chair, threw his feet up onto the desk, pointed at an easel behind him with pictures of the new coinage on it. 'There you are, fellas,' he said, 'That's what they will look like. Anything more you want to know about them?' There was a question or two about the timetable, and the metal to be used, and then I summoned up my courage to ask a question.

'When the old coinage was created there was an international competition and a distinguished panel to pick the best design. How were these selected? Who picked them?'

'We asked the artist to come up with a design, and we liked what she did – I liked them, and the government liked them, so I picked them.'

The young Haughey was nothing but businesslike, and I got the impression he had not much time for competitions, or panels, or indeed, for my question.

I saw more of him when he became Taoiseach and I was covering the thrice-yearly summits of EU heads of state and government. It was during one such summit, in 1982 that I think I really annoyed him. At a press conference in Brussels he made the surprise announcement that he had nominated Fine Gael's Dick Burke to fill the vacancy on the European Commission created earlier by Michael O'Kennedy's resignation to return to Irish political life. Burke, who had previously served a full term as a Commissioner, nominated by the Fine Gael Coalition Government, from 1976 to 1980, was now a Fine Gael Deputy on the Opposition benches.

As the nomination to the Commission was one of the richest patronage plums in the Government's larder, there was amazement that Haughey had now tossed it to a Fine Gael TD who had not been regarded as a particularly successful Commissioner. Making the announcement, he told us that he had nominated Dick Burke 'as the best man available for the job'.

When I got the chance I asked if that phrase meant that Michael O'Kennedy had not been available. O'Kennedy had resigned from the Commission and returned to Irish politics in the expectation that Fianna Fáil would be returned to power in the pending election, and he would have a seat in Government. Haughey had led Fianna Fáil back into power, but O'Kennedy, despite being regarded as a Haugheyite in a divided party, had not been made a Minister and was now languishing on the back benches.

'As I said, Richard Burke is the best man available for the job,' was Haughey's reply.

'Yes, I know you said that, Mr Haughey, but my question was, was Michael O'Kennedy available?

'Look, I am the Taoiseach answering the questions, and I have answered yours.'

'Sorry, I am the journalist asking the question and I still would like to know if Mr O'Kennedy was not available, or if, perhaps, he was not the best man?'

'Next question,' barked a red-faced Taoiseach.

Another meeting arose from a surprise invitation to his mansion at Kinsealy. It was standard practice before a European summit for the Taoiseach to give a briefing to those journalists who would be travelling out to cover it. Normally, this would be on the Friday afternoon, summits being held at weekends. On this particular occasion Mr Haughey had cancelled the Friday briefing, sending a message to us that as the agenda was light and the summit was to be much shorter than usual, he did not think it was necessary to hold one. I was at home on Saturday morning, preparing to travel to Brussels later that evening, when the Taoiseach's office phoned to say there would, after all, be a briefing, and I should be at Kinsealy by noon.

Thus summoned, I drove up to Kinsealy before noon, startling the thoroughbreds in the park, and eager to see inside. I was welcomed at the door by Mrs Haughey, and joined Michael Mills, Chris Glennon and one or two others in the entrance hall. We waited for ten minutes or so, admiring the bronze bust of Mr Haughey, the large painting of Mr Haughey on his horse at the Ward Union meet, a painting of Mr Haughey without his horse, and another of the horse without Mr Haughey. Then he arrived.

'Very good of you to come, fellas,' he greeted us. 'If you come with me we can talk in a little bar I have fixed up at the other end of the house.

It's a traditional pub bar I got down in Roscommon (or Westmeath, or Longford…) and had rebuilt here in the house. I think you'll like it.'

So we followed him through to the reconstructed bar, complete with grand mirror, large mahogany counter, and every imaginable kind of whiskey, beer or stout. We sat down at little round, marble-topped tables, as Charlie started pulling the pints. As I glanced about I saw a series of large line drawings of the 1916 leaders arranged around the frieze above us. Charlie joined us, drawing our attention to the wooden harp presented to him, he said, by the prisoners in Long Kesh. Then swept his hand around the whole installation saying, 'Well, fellas, what do you think of it?' There was a murmur of admiration, and a question or two about it.

'And are all these around the top former barmen?' I asked innocently, pointing to the frieze. 'No, Mr Kennedy, they are not.' He snapped back, and we got on with the briefing. At the end Chris Glennon asked Charlie for a comment on a story in that morning's papers about, I think, unrest in Fianna Fáil.

'Chris,' said Charlie, 'We never see the papers here on a Saturday, so I haven't read the story. I'm entitled to one day a week without the papers.'

We then trooped out, taking a different route towards the front door, so that we could see some more of the house. Mick Mills had a passion for art, and kept stopping to admire some of the fine collection on the walls. He paused at one painting, and exclaimed his liking for it, and for the artist. Charlie was delighted and said he had a couple more by her, just in there in the study, if Mick wanted to have a look.

Mick knew I shared his interest in art, so he nodded to me to join him, and we slipped into the study as Charlie led the others on their tour. Inside the study we saw the paintings, but we also could not avoid noticing the pile of newspapers on the desk – all that morning's, and all thoroughly crumpled and evidently well read.

Another time in Brussels we were summoned to Charlie's hotel suite for a late night chat before the summit commenced the next morning. We were welcomed in the suite by Padraig O'Hanrahan, Haughey's devious but wickedly funny right hand man. 'How's the Taoiseach?' somebody asked. 'Eating children, eating children, so watch out,' replied O'Hanrahan.

As we waited I chatted to Padraig. 'Tell me,' I asked him, 'What have I done to annoy Charlie? He is always totally stiff and formal with me, calls me Mr Kennedy all the time.'

'Don't you know? You never call him Taoiseach, always Mr Haughey. He hates that. You're not showing respect.'

I thought about it, and realised that I never did address him as Taoiseach. There was nothing personal about it – I never called Jack Lynch Taoiseach, nor Garret FitzGerald. Maybe it was my non-conformist dislike of titles, or perhaps impatience with the token use, or abuse, of the Irish language.

The last time I saw Haughey was at Ray Smith's funeral in that large church at Mount Merrion. He was in political disgrace at the time, and slipped into the service by a side door, accompanied by a single companion. I left by the same door at the end, and on my way round to the front saw them, all on their own, heading for the car park. I stopped and said hello, shaking his proffered hand. 'Mr Kennedy,' he murmured.

Garret FitzGerald was a different class of politician. When I joined *The Irish Times* in 1968 he was a Senator, and still writing his weekly economics column in the paper. He was extremely well-versed in EEC affairs, into which I had to read myself very rapidly after Ireland's application for membership became again a live issue. So I saw and heard a lot of him at seminars and meetings, particularly during the long, intense campaign on the 1972 referendum on EEC membership, by which time he had entered the Dáil. I felt I knew him well.

The first time I saw him in action in the Dáil was memorable. I was covering for our Political Correspondent, sitting in the press gallery above the Cean Comhairle as Garret was repeatedly on his feet making points of order and other interventions. As I peered down I saw a Fianna Fáil Deputy from the west walk rather unsteadily into the lobby area behind the tiered benches of the Chamber, evidently on his way back from lunch in the Members' Bar. As many liked to do, instead of taking his seat, he leaned on the back of the uppermost row of benches and surveyed the scene.

After a few minutes, he had had enough of the tousle-headed Garret, and roared across the chamber

'Sit down ya fuzzy-wuzzy FitzGerald. You're up and down like a whoor's knickers.'

I was a bit shocked at the unparliamentary language – Stormont it was not – but have to admit that, thereafter, it was just a tad difficult to take Garret as seriously as he would have liked.

When he became Minister for Foreign Affairs in 1973, he was a different class of Foreign Minister – he had an expert knowledge of European integration and of the institutions and mechanisms of the EEC, and was a serious student of international relations. He did not have to rely on his officials, nor was he troubled by any inferiority complex when dealing with Ministers from other member countries, or with the European Commission.

At the frequent sessions of the EEC Council of Ministers, and later when he accompanied Liam Cosgrave to summits, he was increasingly sought out by non-Irish journalists, particularly British, as a ready source of information on what was going on in the closed meetings – he took copious notes – and his formal briefings, hitherto given to the small Irish press corps, were invaded by other journalists eager to hear his expert analysis of what was, or was not, happening, and why.

Something akin to this was also beginning back in Dublin on the Northern Ireland issue. British press interest in Irish affairs had increased rapidly with the worsening of the violence. The BBC and the London *Times* appointed full time correspondents based in Dublin (John Simpson's BBC career took off with his stint in Ireland) and the *Financial Times* had Dominic Coyle there. These three constituted an *ad hoc* elite press corps, with easy access to Conor Cruise O'Brien, the Government Ministerial spokesman on the North, and to Garret, causing some murmurs of resentment among local journalists.

Certainly Garret made my job in *The Irish Times* much more interesting and challenging. By the time he became Minister in 1973, I had become European Editor, and had also boosted the paper's coverage of development aid, United Nations involvement, Irish foreign policy in general and Irish neutrality in particular. In all these areas Garret was grist to my journalistic mill, while his other great interest, Northern Ireland, chimed with my personal involvement.

In all of them too, his views were what I would have regarded as liberal, or progressive in a general sense, and certainly much more palatable to me personally than those of his predecessor Paddy Hillery, or of any of his successors. Yet over the years I have probably had more private and public differences with Garret, than with any other politician. Some of these arose because I genuinely thought he was mistaken, and told him so, as on Sunningdale and the inclusion of the Council of Ireland, on the New Ireland Forum, which I saw as little more than an exercise in dressing up territorial Nationalism in fancy language, on the need for reform on social issues such as contraception, divorce and abortion, where I thought he was too timid, and on his uncritical support of the so-called peace process with Sinn Féin and the IRA.

But I think I was, like many others, more than a little irritated by Garret the 'know-all', by 'Garret the Good', by Garret 'the Head Boy'. On many topics he knew, not all, but at least a lot more than the rest of us, but it was the way in which, more in sorrow than in anger, he indicated how things would have gone much better if only others had listened to him, that was hardest to take.

He was, for instance, constantly complaining that if the British had been guided by him, there would have been more progress in the North, or blandly asserting that 'we', meaning the Irish Government and people, understood the North far better than the British could ever hope to. To someone like me, highly critical of Dublin's limited grasp of the Northern issue, listening to such assertions was bad for the blood pressure. London constantly made mistakes in Northern Ireland, but its misreading of the problem was not helped by an equally, if not more, erroneous analysis coming from Dublin.

Every time Garret cited his Belfast Presbyterian mother as proof positive of his own insight into Unionism, I could not help reflecting to myself that a Belfast Presbyterian who had embraced both violent twentieth-century Republicanism and, eventually, Catholicism, was not the most reliable conduit to an understanding of the Northern mind, even if she was your mother.

I once asked a German journalist friend who was close to Chancellor Helmut Schmidt what Schmidt thought of Garret. (During his eight years as Chancellor, Schmidt would have encountered Garret, as Minister and as Taoiseach, at many EEC meetings.) My friend said he did not know, but he would ask. He did; Schmidt, he said, had been polite, and said Mr FitzGerald was very good, but added that he (Schmidt) did not like being lectured to. 'Mr FitzGerald is a man for the trees. I prefer the forest.'

Shortly after I was appointed Diplomatic Correspondent in 1969 I was invited to a lunch at Lucan House, the residence of the Italian Ambassador, and the most beautiful of all diplomatic residences in Dublin. I was seated near the end of a long table, close to a window looking out onto a garden bathed in sunshine. That vision was soon eclipsed when the most elegant, beautifully dressed young lady took the seat directly opposite me. It was Mary Bourke, Reid Professor of Law at Trinity.

Our paths were to cross frequently over the years. When my friend and colleague John Horgan was elected to the Senate in 1969, he and Senator Mary Robinson (as she became in 1970) formed the vanguard of a movement for social reform, particularly relating to contraception and divorce, so I met her fairly often when I was John's guest for lunch in Leinster House. I saw even more of her during the 1972 referendum campaign, and more still after Ireland joined the EEC in 1973.

Later she took a courageous and, to me, enlightened stance against the Anglo-Irish Agreement. We remained in touch even after I had left *The Irish Times* in 1985. On a range of issues – social reform, Europe, Northern Ireland – she reflected my own views more closely than almost any other Southern politician. But no politician is perfect, and I began to have my doubts about Mary when she danced away with the fairies in her inauguration speech as President in 1990. Her Presidential blessing on Gerry Adams, by way of that handshake in West Belfast in June 1993, well before the first IRA ceasefire, further tarnished the golden image I had had of her from that first sunny day in Lucan.

Noel Browne I had known about since my student days in the 1950s, travelling down to debates in Dublin. There, people I met, like David Thornley and Owen Dudley Edwards, were worshippers at the feet of the austere Dr Browne. I first met the man himself, oddly enough, in the bowels of Maynooth. With John Horgan, I was invited to a little caucus in the rooms of the Professor of Moral Theology, Enda MacDonagh, which included, among one or two others, Dr Noel Browne. I was not sure which to be more impressed by, meeting Noel Browne, or getting inside Maynooth.

It was, I think, about 1969, and we were there, not to set the world to rights, but to tackle something much more difficult – how to move Ireland into the twentieth century. Thereafter I met Noel Browne over lunch several times in the Dáil. It was during his Labour Party phase, when his wisdom was still triumphing over his eccentricity.

I first encountered Conor Cruise O'Brien in the 1950s, when, as a student at Queen's in Belfast, I had gone to hear him speaking at the annual student debate on Partition. He was there as Head of the Irish News Agency to champion the cause of irredentist Irish Nationalism. He soon got over all that, and when I next heard his voice in 1969 – he had just returned to Ireland after several years in New York – it was among the sanest on the island on partition and most other things.

That was in his ex-father-in-law's house on the Ravenhill Road in Belfast. I had been sent North to assist our Northern editor, Fergus Pyle, for a few days, and Conor had asked some journalists to meet him to discuss the civil rights agitation. His analysis of what was happening, and where it might be heading, was mightily impressive, and proved, sadly, very accurate. I can't remember a word he said in the 1950s student debate, but I can almost every word of that 1969 conversation.

Conor's great friend within *The Irish Times,* was Michael MacInerney, and I was to meet Conor again in Michael's flat on several occasions. The two men had developed great mutual respect; Michael was from a working class Limerick background and had been involved in Republicanism and communism in the 1930s as a member of the Connolly Association in London and editor of the *Irish Democrat.* A long-time socialist, he had moved to total rejection of political violence, and shared Conor's abhorrence of the IRA and all its works.

Conor's great enemy in *The Irish Times* was, of course, Douglas Gageby. They had known each other in pre-war Trinity days, where Conor had for a time been Gageby's tutor, and also the Trinity Correspondent of *The Irish Times.* The two had worked together on the Irish News Agency in the 1950s where Conor had been managing director, and Gageby editor-in-chief. But since those days, Conor had not only stopped preaching Nationalism, he had become its foremost intellectual challenger.

When he later became a regular columnist in *The Irish Times,* the weekly arrival of his column in proof form on Gageby's desk was usually greeted with a sigh of 'Bloody Conor, I suppose I'd better read it.' Generally, he hated it, and at one stage I found myself called in to mediate between the two when the column was cut, or held out on legal advice, and Conor took umbrage.

Douglas asked me to phone Conor. 'I can't talk to him, I'll only lose my temper. But you get on with him. Ring him and try to calm him down. He might listen to you,' he said, making it sound as if this indicated some serious character defect on my part. I took it as the highest compliment he ever paid me.

For years at dinner parties around Dublin I found the best way to enliven flagging conversation was to postulate the view that Conor Cruise O'Brien was the greatest living Irishman. The discussion became really heated when the others realised I meant it.

No one ever made such a claim on behalf of Paddy Hillery, nor would he, in his wildest dreams, have claimed it for himself. But of all the politicians I had to deal with in Dublin, he was the one I liked best, the one with whom, personally, I felt most at ease. Yet we had almost nothing in common. He was from Clare and had seen almost nothing of the North until an official drove him in a Murray rental car on a clandestine visit to Belfast in 1970. He was Fianna Fáil, a party towards which I had a congenital antipathy. He displayed little of the sharp intellect of an O'Brien, nor the broad knowledge of a FitzGerald, nor much sign of immersion in things cultural. (Though he did paint.)

In politics we agreed on almost nothing. Most of our many conversations, certainly in the years immediately following our first marathon one on the Northern question in Iveagh House in 1969, consisted of heated arguments, over Articles 1, 2, and 3 of Bunreacht na hEireann; over the need to reform the laws on contraception; censorship; abortion; divorce; the Irish language; and a lot more.

He was no die-hard on most of these issues, and our arguments generally ended with him reminding me that politics was the art of the possible, and me countering that that was a tired cliché, and the real art of politics was making things possible. We continued these arguments after he moved to be a European Commissioner in Brussels, and even after he became President, though in much more relaxed mode. I was from time to time invited up to Áras an Uachtaráin for a private lunch with him.

Like most Presidents he was lonely and isolated in the Park, but I think he felt it more, having been snatched from the intensity of a high-powered job in Brussels, right at the centre of a whole new chapter in European and Irish political history. As President he had little to do, which was just as well, as he had neither the staff nor the resources to do anything.

But he was interested in people, in how they behaved, in their motivations, in how their personalities affected their actions. At one level this could be dismissed as not much more than a love of gossip, but in his case it was informed by his medical background and his knowledge of psychiatry.

I remember being at a crowded Government reception in some grand venue in the early seventies. I was standing on my own at the edge of the throng when I was poked in the ribs. 'Look at Jack, look at Jack. What's he thinking?' It was Paddy Hillery, and he was pointing across the room to where the Taoiseach, Jack Lynch, was standing on his own, head and shoulders above most of the mob, one arm on an elegant mantelpiece, quietly puffing his pipe and gazing into the middle distance. I laughed and said I had no idea what he was thinking. Paddy replied:

'That's the thing; you never know with Jack. He's a deep one.'

About the same period I had an appointment with the Minister in Iveagh House. As I was shown into his office, before I could even sit down, he began: 'What's Blaney up to?' I was mystified and replied that I had no idea, that he was in the same Cabinet and should know better than me what his fellow Minister was doing. He dismissed the subject, saying Blaney was up to something on the North, and he thought I might have heard of it. The conversation made more sense when the arms crisis broke a few weeks later and Blaney was sacked on suspicion of involvement in the plot.

Paddy Hillery was in some ways an accidental politician. He had been persuaded by De Valera to stand for the party in Clare in 1951, as Dev's running mate, and went on to gain respect as a good departmental minister in various posts. When Lemass was retiring as party leader in 1966, Hillery was one of several ministers he encouraged to go forward as his successor. Hillery said no. While he was a most conscientious departmental minister – and was proud of his achievements in Education and Labour – I doubt he ever wanted the top job.

His time in Foreign Affairs, from 1969 to the end of 1972, was dominated, not by the erupting Northern crisis, but by the negotiation of EEC membership. In his handling of that he contributed to a minor revolution in relations between press and government. Because the negotiation was prolonged and complicated, because the substance of it involved much technical detail, and because, at the end, the outcome had to be submitted to referendum, the journalists covering it were offered regular and systematic, and confidential, briefings on all the issues, by both the minister and his senior departmental officials. (I still have files of documents marked 'Confidential', or 'Speaking notes for the Minister'.)

This was, for Foreign Affairs, a revolution, and not a minor one. Up to 1969 Frank Aiken, the long-term custodian of Ireland's external affairs, had been reluctant to allow the Dáil, never mind the press, to probe into the mysteries of Irish foreign policy. Elsewhere in government, journalists were often enough on close personal terms with ministers and by that means privy to much of what went on inside government, but Hillery was something of a pioneer in putting some structure on that relationship, and ensuring that key civil servants were involved, and made themselves accessible to the press.

His role on Northern Ireland was limited by the fact that others in the Government, from the Taoiseach down, were deeply involved in it. In his public speeches he did little more than follow the traditional Fianna Fáil line as slightly modernised by Sean Lemass. Had he been longer in Iveagh House, and had the EEC not monopolised most of his time and attention, he might have contributed some fresh ideas and innovative thinking on the North.

Certainly he did not share the Government's seemingly blind admiration for the SDLP, nor did he assume that their approach and analysis was infallible. More than once he remarked to me in private that he wished the SDLP would stop running down to Dublin to complain to the Government. They would be better to stay at home, he suggested, and learn to deal with the Unionists, or go to London where ultimate responsibility lay. This suggested less than rigid commitment to one key feature of the Government's Northern policy at that time, and right up to the Anglo-Irish Agreement in 1985 - insistence on Dublin's right to represent and speak for the Nationalist minority in Northern Ireland.

Paddy Hillery was never, I felt, a gut Fianna Fáil man, which is perhaps why we got on so well.

He was, ironically, ill-served by the press when the rumours of scandal hit the Presidency in 1979. When he learned that a Brussels newspaper was reporting that his marriage was in jeopardy, that he had a long-term mistress, acquired while he was a European Commissioner, and that the English Sunday papers were about to run the story, he immediately consulted the Taoiseach, Jack Lynch. Lynch told him to call in the editors of the papers and RTE, and talk to them in confidence about the matter. This he did, and the editors, led I believe by Douglas Gageby, said he should call in the Political Correspondents and make a statement to them.

This ensured that the story was made public, albeit in the form of a complete denial. So the detailed rumours of the affair were publicised, and read much more avidly by the citizens of Ireland than the denial, and, sad to say, probably more widely believed. Hillery continued to insist, publicly and privately, that there was no truth whatsoever in the story. I believed him.

But for the alleged scandal, he would probably not have served a second term as president. He was reluctant to do so, but was persuaded that refusing to accept nomination for a second term would be tantamount to an admission that the rumours were true, or would be taken as such.

Another friend, John Hume, comes into a rather different category from the others in that he was a Northern politician. I had known him from Derry in 1963, when he had come to prominence as a leading figure in the campaign to bring the proposed new university to that city. I had liked him then, and got to know him much better during my regular trips North to cover the civil rights marches after 1968. In the 1970s he was one of the regular stream of visitors I used to meet in Gageby's office, and though we never agreed totally on all things, we became friends.

We argued still more after he began leading the SDLP up what seemed, to me, an ever greener path, but we never fell out. We did agree on most things European, and after his election to the European Parliament in 1979 I saw him frequently in Strasbourg and Brussels. In 1985 he was influential in persuading me to return to Belfast as head of the European Commission office there.

Eighteen

Friendly Fergus

One fine day in June 1974 I arrived into the office just after lunch to be greeted, as I passed his desk, by a shell-shocked Donal Foley. He took me aside and said 'Douglas is gone. Fergus is the editor. He'll be taking the five o'clock conference. It was announced at the twelve o'clock.'

A change of editor in any newspaper has an impact that is perhaps difficult to appreciate for people in other lines of business. The editor, particularly in a smallish paper like *The Irish Times,* is the supreme boss, but not some remote authority. Every journalist works to him; his relationship with the editor is the most significant factor in his working life, for good or ill.

When an editor has been in post for a decade, and when he has been as dominant a personality as Douglas Gageby, his abrupt departure without any hint or warning is an earthquake. When his successor, almost miraculously, is in his seat within hours, without consultation, it begins to feel like an earthquake followed by a revolution.

The reaction to Fergus Pyle's appointment, across the editorial department, was initially shock, compounded by insecurity and followed, very quickly, by resentment. The resentment resulted from the manner of the change. The lack of any consultation, of any process of selecting a new editor, was a stark reminder to the journalists, even the most senior, that, whatever they thought, they were not the paper, they were merely employees who helped bring it out every day. The new editor had been imposed by the departing editor and the shadowy but ever-present chairman, the Major.

Unfairly, much of this resentment was soon attached to the new editor; unfairly because the appointment had been as much a shock to him as to the rest of us, and he had, at first, protested his unfitness for the appointment, and even asked for the cup to be passed from him.

To many on the staff he was relatively unknown, other than as a name in the paper. He had last worked in Dublin in 1966, not as a reporter or a sub, but as features editor. In that year Gageby had decided to open a Belfast office, and Fergus had been sent to staff it. In 1969 Gageby wanted to put a staff man in Paris, and Fergus moved from Belfast direct to Paris. In 1972, he transferred to Brussels, where we were opening an office following acceptance of Irish membership of the EEC, and he was still there in June 1974 when the call came to be editor.

So for eight years he had not been working in the Dublin office. The paper had changed a lot in those years, and there had been many newcomers to the staff. Only the older, more long-serving members knew him personally, plus those who had, in 1968 and 1969, been shuttling North on a regular basis to assist in coverage of the Troubles. That was how I had first met him. Then, after his move to Paris, my role as Diplomatic Correspondent and chief reporter of all things European meant I saw him more frequently. Since we had opened the Brussels office in mid-1972 I had, as European Editor, been in touch with him daily, and was, theoretically at least, his superior, though that was not really the way The Irish Times worked.

I probably knew him better at a personal level than most others in the Dublin office, and while I had to digest the thought that I was now working for the person who had, in a sense, been working for me the previous day, that was made easier by the fact that I liked Fergus, admired his intellect, his broad range of knowledge and his ability as a journalist, and that we had become good friends.

Not everyone shared my high opinion of him. To sub-editors in particular he was a problem at the end of a phone. He took a very flexible attitude towards deadlines, and never felt under any great obligation to limit his copy to the length agreed earlier in the day. So to a number of subs he was that fellow in Belfast, Paris or Brussels who was invariably late with his copy, and never knew when to stop. That was bad enough, but Gageby had established, right from his first days in Belfast, that Fergus' copy was, if not sacrosanct, at least to be treated with much respect. So any sub tempted to put manners on Fergus by butchering his copy, or even leaving it out, was certain to incur the wrath of the editor. Then, to have this man, whom they were accustomed to belittle and moan about on a daily basis, suddenly thrust into the seat of supreme power, was more than they could forgive.

But it was the manner of his appointment that harmed Fergus most. In many ways he was an obvious successor to Gageby, and had probably been identified as such for some time by both Douglas and the Major. He was well-educated, highly intelligent, non-controversial in his politics, about the right age, and long established in the paper. He was also a Southern Protestant, but I would doubt if this was, as some have suggested, the deciding factor. Rather he was appointed because he was socially, intellectually, and in terms of his education and other ways, an *Irish Times* type. Being Protestant was no disqualification, but by 1974 it was no longer the distinguishing mark of an *Irish Times* man.

Both Douglas and the Major no doubt considered Fergus' years in Belfast, Paris and Brussels as excellent preparation for the editorship, and assumed that appointing him was the surest way to guarantee a smooth transition. It is a measure of their authoritarian management of the paper that neither man even considered consultation with the staff, let alone the unions, and that it never occurred to them that, by acting as they did, they ensured that, from day one, Fergus had enemies within the camp.

A change of style was inevitable after Gageby. Fergus was affable, enthusiastic and less than organised. Unlike the ever-spruce Gageby, there was a comfortable disorder in his dress. I had first met him in Belfast shortly after I joined the paper in 1968; I had come up to help cover a civil rights march, and we went together to a briefing. I still remember him taking lengthy, long-hand notes, not in a note-book, but all around the margins of that day's *Irish Times*, which had been tucked under his arm.

He was also very talkative. I have a vivid memory of being driven back to Brussels by him from a meeting in Luxembourg, with two other journalists. Fergus tackled driving as he did much else, with enthusiasm and some disregard for strict observance of the rules. It was dark, and the route was not yet the motorway it was to become. As well as driving, Fergus was dominating the conversation, which meant repeatedly half-turning his head to respond to the two in the back seat. I was in the front, keeping an eye on the road, and as we entered an improved stretch I suddenly realised that Fergus was taking a branch off the main carriageway, so I said hey, we should have gone on straight. Without breaking off what he was saying to the rear seat, he swerved onto the rough ground between the carriageway and the slip road, slowed to a stop, reversed a bit, and, bumping and bouncing, regained the main carriageway – still in full spate to the back-benchers.

His love of talking meant one change from the Gageby regime was immediately apparent: editorial conferences lasted a great deal longer than before. This was not just because he liked talking, but because he genuinely wanted to associate others with the editing of the paper. I think he was aware of the lack of enthusiasm among sections of the staff for his appointment, and that, in any event, he could not have the instant personal authority of his predecessor.

But rambling, over-long, editorial conferences do not fit easily into a newspaper's daily routine, and in Fergus' case they probably further alienated those who had not taken kindly to his appointment, and tried the patience of those who were happy to work with him.

Shortly after his appointment Fergus, possibly at the prompting of the Major, made a significant change in the way the paper was edited, and how the editor's office was run. He appointed two new Assistant Editors to work in his office, and to share the nightly task of editing the paper in its later stages of production – which meant being there until the city edition had gone to press, and possibly to two or three in the morning, or sometimes later. The two appointees were Jim Downey and myself; me possibly because Fergus had already worked closely with me without any problems, and because European and foreign policy affairs generally were looming larger in the paper, and Jim, I suspect, not just because of his long experience as a sub, working on the actual putting together of the paper, or his considerable knowledge of domestic politics, but because Fergus was probably aware that Jim had not been overjoyed at the choice of new editor, and this was an attempt to win him to his side.

One by-product of this move, as far as I was concerned, was that it brought me into constant contact with Bruce Williamson, who was to become my closest friend in the *Irish Times* for the rest of my time there, dispensing to me, on a daily basis, chocolate doughnuts, wise council, numerous books and a wealth of information on literature, films and much else.

Under Fergus there was more discussion of how the paper should be run, what it should say, how it could be improved. These discussions usually concluded, not with anything being decided, but because we had run out of time. After one such eminently inconclusive debate, I suggested to Fergus that it might be a good idea if he wound up meetings with his own summary of what had been decided, and indicated what should now be done, and by whom.

He smiled at me and said no, that was not the way to handle things. We were all experienced journalists, we knew our jobs, and the discussion was what mattered – everyone had had his say, and everyone had gone away knowing what had to be done. I should learn to trust people more.

There was also much more discussion of editorial policy, and of lines to be taken in particular leaders. I joined with a will in any debate on the line we should take on Northern Ireland and the continuing violence. At one long session I cited a number of recent leading articles and pointed out that in all of them we were saying what London should do about the North, never what our own Government could contribute. I suggested advocating stronger action against the IRA, easier extradition, social reform in the South, removal of the constitutional claim to the North, and the like.

The discussion rambled on, and as time ran out, Fergus, for once, made a decision. It was a good idea, he said, and he asked one of my senior colleagues to have a go at it. I was away for a couple of days and did not see the resulting editorial until it was in print. It laid out in detail what our Government should do – it should press London to do A, persuade London to do B, and get Brussels and Washington to lean on London to do C. A, B, and C being the same things that our earlier editorials had been saying London should do.

Unlike Gageby, Fergus could, at times, be persuaded to take a clear party political line at elections. When the 1977 general election was called, after four years of Fine Gael-Labour coalition, some of us persuaded Fergus that we should not come out for either the Coalition or Fianna Fáil, but instead should argue the case that a vote for the Labour Party was the best way to move forward, away from the politics of the civil war.

I was deputed to write the leader, and spent a day perfecting my arguments and polishing my logic. It was published with little editing. The Coalition lost the election, Labour lost two seats and about 15% of its vote. Shortly afterwards Fergus lost his job, but that had nothing to do with backing Labour.

It was the Arabs who did for him. The first big oil shock of the seventies had come in 1973, but its disastrous economic consequences really hit Ireland in the middle of 1974, just as Fergus was catapulted into the editor's chair. It was hard times all round, and advertising revenue began to fall dramatically. The collapse of the Sunningdale power-sharing executive in Northern Ireland had already added its own layer of gloom, as bitter stalemate replaced hope. There was a shortage of good news, as well as of petrol.

For the decade up to 1975, the circulation of *The Irish Times* had been growing strongly, while that of *The Irish Press* had been declining, and the *Independent* remaining almost static. By 1976 it was clear that not only had the growth at the *Times* stopped, it was actually losing circulation, while the other two were holding their sales, or even increasing them slightly in the case of the *Press*. This, coupled with the sharp drop in advertising revenue was enough to spread an air of crisis around *The Irish Times*.

Among the journalists, the backstairs criticism of Fergus grew, led by those who had never been reconciled to his appointment. But his most determined opponent turned out to be Andrew Whittaker, who had moved from being an energetic and well regarded Business Editor, to a post in the Major's administration end of the business, rising eventually to be Assistant General Manager. One of his remits at that time was the vigorous promotion of the paper, through advertising on radio and other methods, as a means of regaining circulation.

Perhaps it was that perspective that convinced Whittaker that the key to the paper's salvation, never mind recovery, was the removal of Fergus. By his own account, in *Bright, Brilliant Days*, his 2007 book on *The Irish Times*, he had, as early as mid-1976, advised the Major that Fergus had to go. He also sought support from senior journalists for a concerted effort to remove the editor. I had known and liked Andrew from my first contacts with him when I had joined the paper, and we generally saw eye to eye on most things, but when he approached me privately, in late '76 or early '77, to give my backing to an editorial approach to management to have Fergus removed, I refused.

My immediate response was that Fergus had appointed me as one of his Assistant Editors, and that my loyalty was to him. Andrew told me that my loyalty had to be to the paper, not any one individual, and we had a sharp exchange. I had no real answer to his claims that Fergus was vague and indecisive, that he was not a born editor in the style of Gageby, and that he had lost the support of at least some of his senior staff, but I felt it was grossly unfair to blame him for the crisis in the paper. The loss in advertising revenue was due to external events and the oil crisis, exacerbated by serious weaknesses in the management of the paper, and mistakes in attempts to diversify, none of which could be laid at the editor's door.

Nor was I convinced that the drop in circulation was directly linked to the change of editor. When the hard times hit, *The Irish Times'* circulation had been increasing rapidly over most of a decade; many of its readers, indeed most of them, were new readers, and therefore less likely to stick with the paper. In all the criticism that I had heard of Fergus' style of editing, no one had produced evidence to convince me that this had been reflected in any radical change in the policy, content or general approach of the paper itself. One monument to his credit still stands – he brought Martyn Turner into the paper as a full-time cartoonist, something it had never had before. Martyn, then based in Northern Ireland, had been contributing regular cartoons to the paper, but Fergus – at my suggestion – agreed a contract that meant daily cartoons and

A 1985 caricature of author by Martyn Turner.

enabled Martyn to move house, family, dogs, and Eric the goat South.

But between 1973 and 1977 *The Irish Times* sales dropped by more than 7%, unlike those of the *Press* and *Independent*.

When the chapel of the NUJ met in early 1977 to debate a motion to approach management to indicate loss of confidence in the editor, I spoke passionately against it. I said it was entirely inappropriate for journalists to go running to management behind their editor's back. Their loyalty was to their editor. I was, as far as I remember, the only person in the crowded meeting to speak against the motion. When it came to a vote, one colleague voted with me, and another abstained. The rest endorsed the move.

I did not know then that senior journalists had gone first to Douglas Gageby, who, though retired, was still a member of *The Irish Times* board, to complain about Fergus and discuss how he could be removed. It was a dirty business. I still think that without the oil crisis, the world recession and shortcomings in the business management of the paper, Fergus could have ambled through a full term as editor, despite the resentment attaching to the manner of his appointment.

Much is made of Douglas Gageby's rescue of the paper after his return in 1977. From 1978 things certainly got better, and the circulation did recover dramatically. But the *Independent*, and ailing *Press*, also enjoyed remarkable increases in circulation in those same years, and neither of them had any Gageby factor to benefit from.

After some years in a stop-gap information job in Trinity College, Fergus swallowed his pride, showed considerable courage, and came back to the paper he had once edited, to work, as a writing journalist, for the two men who had fired him: the Major and Douglas. Before his tragically early death in 1997, he was to produce his best journalism.

Nineteen

Diplomats at Home

The Swiss are an honest, kindly, neutral people, not renowned for their wit and repartee. The Swiss Ambassador was a true representative of his nation, and the lunch at his residence in Dublin was proceeding in a very Swiss vein of polite but stilted conversation. At the head of the table His Excellency was manning his post, doing his best to steer the dozen or so of us around it away from the gaping holes of silence which repeatedly threatened to derail the occasion.

A lady sitting opposite me had just confessed, under questioning from HE, that she was from Limerick. The Ambassador seized upon this as a drowning man would a lifebelt, and inquired of us generally if we knew how the term limerick had come to be applied to a firmly structured five-line poetic format in the English language. No one did, and after another five minutes of carefully studying our cutlery, it was clear that no one cared.

At which point the man from the Department of Foreign Affairs showed his mettle. 'I know a limerick,' he informed the table, and proceeded as follows,

> Il y avait un jeune homme de Dijon
> Qui ne croyait que peu de religion
> Il criait à haute voix :
> Je hais tous les trois
> Le père, et le fils, et le pigeon.

A few seconds of shocked silence were followed by extremely un-Swiss gales of laughter, and suddenly everyone knew a limerick, and not all of them of the high spiritual content of that one. The lunch went famously, though I am not sure if the Ambassador marked it down as a triumph or a disaster; come to think of it, that was the first and last lunch I was ever invited to at the Swiss embassy.

The man from the Department was Sean Gaynor. I had met him when I was first appointed Diplomatic Correspondent, and Frank Aiken still owned the Department and ran it as a private fief. Sean had soldiered with Aiken on many excursions, and delighted in telling tales out of school, of how, for instance, Aiken, the redoubtable Republican from South Armagh, had resolutely defended Ireland's Catholic honour on the dangerous ground of votes relating to population control i.e. contraception, at the World Population Conference in Teheran. (He had sent Sean round to the Holy See delegation to ask how they were voting.)

It was from Sean that I learned about another side entirely to the stern Aiken: Aiken the inventor of the Inflatable Boot. Aiken, it seemed, was a keen dabbler in things scientific and mechanical, and had designed this boot as an aid to the army. Once inflated, the boot enabled an infantry man to bounce his way forward at a significantly faster rate, or that was the theory. Sean also told me to look out for the small windmill Aiken had designed and built to generate power at his home in Sandyford. For years after I could not drive along the Hillcrest Road without peering through the trees to catch a reassuring glance of the Aiken windmill.

Sean himself had a mechanical bent, and was a master, not just of the limerick form, but of the internal combustion engine. When he was appointed to his first ambassadorial post, his immediate request to Iveagh House was for permission to service the Mercedes himself. He was a delightful man, and the first of my many good friends in the Department.

Lunches and dinners at the Dublin Embassies were a small but agreeable part of the Diplomatic Correspondent's work. As protocol seemed to dictate that there had to be one guest from Foreign Affairs, this gave me a chance to get to know officials I might not have otherwise encountered. In those early days there were not many above a dozen or so resident embassies, not all of them particularly active, and not all of whom would ever have deigned to invite any journalist under the rank of editor-in-chief to their Ambassadorial table.

Thus, in all my decade and a half in charge of *Irish Times* foreign and diplomatic coverage, I was never once invited to lunch or dinner at the American Ambassador's residence, nor, less surprisingly perhaps, to any function at the Papal Nuncio's retreat in the Phoenix Park, though the Nuncio was permanent Dean of the Diplomatic Corps. The British Ambassador's stately Glencairn, on the other hand, was familiar territory, while Dutch, French, Indian, Spanish, Italian and Canadian ambassadors were hospitable, as was, later, the Greek.

American ambassadors to Ireland were invariably political appointees, not career diplomats, and tended to leave the real work of the embassy to the professionals. This meant that it was Dublin high society which beat a path to the residence in the Phoenix Park, while the task of wining and dining journalists, and pumping them for information, was left to underlings, particularly to the Political Officer, known to us as 'the spook'.

All foreign diplomats loved *The Irish Times,* and took it as their gospel on all things Irish. About six months after becoming Diplomatic Correspondent, I was invited to an Ambassadorial lunch, and set off flushed with pride at just having had published a two-part analysis of Irish foreign policy. My neighbour at the table was an elegant lady married to a diplomat from another embassy. When she heard I was from *The Irish Times* she was fulsome in her praise of it, particularly its coverage of Ireland's foreign relations. She read it every day. What was my name again, she asked. I told her, and she looked puzzled. 'Do you write under your own name?' she asked. Somewhat deflated, I confessed that I did, and she seemed even more puzzled.

At dinners the old conventions were strictly observed. After dessert the ladies would withdraw, led by the ambassador's wife, to some undisclosed destination, while the gentlemen gathered round the Ambassador at the head of the table for port, cigars and serious consideration of matters political. This formula was adhered to, even when the female guests might include a serving diplomat from another embassy.

Marie Cecile Schulte-Strathaus was an elegant and somewhat formal lady of a certain age who was both Cultural Attaché and Information Officer at the German Embassy. I seem to remember that she was also, for a short time between Ambassadors, Chargé d'Affaires. I can still see the look of incredulity on her face when, as we sat talking at a dinner at the Dutch Ambassador's residence, the Ambassador's wife briskly whisked her away with the ladies. Even more outraged was a young, recently elected TD, Miss Síle De Valera, when she too was invited to join the ladies and leave the men to their weighty discussion.

Diplomatic lunches were very agreeable, at least for some of those present. For people like myself, or the Man from the Department, or indeed our host, they were work. We were there only because it was part of our job, and there was therefore no pressure on us to rush back to work, as we were already working. Lunch could go on, if not for ever, then at least until well into the afternoon. At lunch there was none of the nonsense of the ladies withdrawing. Instead we would all withdraw from the table and settle into comfortable chairs for our postprandials. Others from the world of commerce might feel obliged to tear themselves away between 2.30 and 3.00, pleading a meeting, or a heavy afternoon, and there was always a danger that if enough of them left we might not have a quorum, and the lunch would collapse.

One particularly convivial Man from the Department had perfected a technique to avert any such misfortune. The crucial moment would come if, at say 2.45pm, three or four guests would set aside their glasses, rise to their feet and express their regrets that they simply had to go. Politeness required that all remaining gentlemen would rise too, and having got so far some would be tempted to follow tamely towards the exit. At which point our Man from the Department would collapse noisily into his armchair, and inquire loudly if anyone would join him in another Cognac. It was a magic formula which never failed.

It must have been after one such intervention that I found myself in conversation with China's first, newly arrived, Ambassador to Ireland, the harmoniously named Madame Gong. Discovering I was from *The Irish Times,* she delivered the customary eulogy of that paper and all its works, and then went on to say it carried remarkably perceptive editorials on China, which seemed to be the work of a real expert. How did we do it?

I did not know what to say. It was true we did indeed carry regular leaders on China, all written by Bruce Williamson, who had probably never been inside a Chinese restaurant, let alone China. Bruce, at Gageby's request, wrote a leader almost every day on some foreign topic or other. I was never sure whether this was simply to fill the space, or to convince our readers that we were a serious newspaper with an international outlook. One reason for picking China was probably because it was very far away, very few of our readers would know anything about it, and we did not have to go out on any limbs over it.

Another reason was that Bruce was quite interested in it. All his foreign knowledge was gleaned from a lifetime of reading the *Economist,* the *Times* and *The Guardian*, and listening to the BBC World Service, so he was up-to-date on things Chinese. He was also a very intelligent man who wrote well, so it was not too surprising that Madame Gong assumed we had a hot line to Peking.

But I was not going to try to explain all that. Besides I knew the Chinese regime's official line on the western consensus on China – which was what our editorials were reflecting – was to denounce it as the propaganda of running dogs, and that Madame Gong was just pumping me for information. So, fortified by the brandy perhaps, I told her that the editorials were written by specialists, who came to us as part of a unique day-release scheme we operated with a large Dublin institution known as Grangegorman.

I was beginning to elaborate on this when I was saved from myself by another of the guests bursting into laughter and explaining to Madame Gong that this was a joke, and telling her the true function of Grangegorman.

She smiled a totally inscrutable smile and turned to talk to someone else. Bruce thought it was rather funny when I told him about it.

Twenty

The Good Old Times

The Irish Times I first fell in love with was the pre-Gageby paper. I had started reading it as a student in Belfast in the mid-1950s, and was a daily communicant from 1959 onwards, that is four years before Douglas became editor. It may well have been the paper of the fast dwindling Protestant minority in the South, with an equally fast-dwindling circulation, but I bought it because it had a personality all of its own, and because it contained what, to me, were wonderful nuggets of original, eccentric and downright funny writing. It was unmistakably Irish, but never parochially or provincially so.

He was gone before I became a reader, but I think Patrick Campbell's Quidnunc columns of the 1940s, in which he daintily trod a precarious path between whimsy and total nonsense to portray a lifestyle that was both carefree and constantly threatened with disaster, give a flavour of what was a unique newspaper. In the same league, or rather in a similar one all of his own, was Myles na gCopaleen, whose Cruiskeen Lawn was running when I started reading the paper regularly.

It was part of Douglas Gageby's achievement that, in a different Ireland at a different time, he helped rescue the paper from commercial extinction while maintaining enough of that flavour, of that quirky personality, to retain its distinctiveness. There is still, if you look hard enough, an echo of that delightful quirkiness in the twenty-first century *Irish Times*, but not a lot. Pre-Gageby, it had already established itself as a liberal outpost in an oppressively conservative country. It had fought battles against censorship, against the Fethard-on-Sea boycott in 1957, and had taken some healthy swipes at the autocratic John Charles McQuade, the Catholic Archbishop of Dublin. Before that it had, unlike the rest of the Dublin press, looked sympathetically on the Republican side in the Spanish Civil War.

When I joined in 1968, Douglas had been in the editorial chair for five years, so he had put his own stamp upon the paper. But there were still around the office many reminders of past days, apart from the portrait of R. M. Smyllie above the editor's chair. Bruce Williamson, later to become my closest friend and counsellor; Ken Gray; Donal O'Donovan; Terence de Vere White; Seamus Kelly; Noel Fee; and Fergus Pyle (then in Belfast) all dated from the time of Alec Newman's editorship, and in Bruce's case, from that of Smyllie. Lionel Flemming, known to all as Bill, dated back even further. He had originally joined the paper when John Healy was editor, and Smyllie his assistant.

It was still possible to detect, in odd bits of conversation, some wounds and ill-feelings from the sacking of Newman in 1961, for which Douglas, then managing director, was generally held responsible. But that was a long time ago, and Bruce Williamson, who had resigned in protest at Newman's sacking, had been brought back into the paper by Douglas and reinstated as Deputy Editor.

The recovery in circulation had begun, though it was still the smallest of the Dublin dailies. Michael Viney's numerous series analysing and often criticising many aspects of Irish life and society, plus Fergus Pyle's extensive reporting on Northern Ireland and John Horgan's despatches from Vatican II had all helped make *The Irish Times* increasingly required reading for the rising Dublin middle and business and professional classes – most of them Catholic. Seamus Kelly, Terence de Vere White and Charles Acton were the staple diet for devotees of theatre, literature and music. Michael McInerney and John Healy produced the prescribed texts for the followers of politics, as did Paul MacWeeney for the rugby fraternity, and Paddy Downey for the Gaels.

And there was Hoddy for the jazz lovers. I had been on the staff of the paper for about six months, when, first in on a Sunday morning about ten o'clock, I had been startled by the sight of a disreputable looking bearded individual, badly dressed with a duffle bag over his shoulder, shuffling across the newsroom from the direction of the gents lavatory. He bade me a gruff good morning and disappeared. When Donal Foley arrived in later, I said I thought there had been a tramp of some sort sleeping overnight in the office, and described the intruder.

'Oh, that's Hoddy,' said Donal, 'Our distinguished jazz correspondent, otherwise George D. Hodnett. He often spends the night in the office, indeed I sometimes think he lives here.'

Hoddy, I learned, whatever his appearance and his sleeping arrangements, was a jazz pianist of high reputation and the son of a distinguished military man. He had grown up in Frescati, the one-time residence in Blackrock of Lord Edward FitzGerald, and had studied law at Trinity.

I was never to be on more than nodding terms with Hoddy, but he was my first indication of a shadowy, wider *Irish Times* of which we staff journalists were only a part. Far better known outside the office than in it, were our Bridge Correspondent, our Insurance Correspondent, our Banking Correspondent, several churches correspondents and goodness knows who else. They were not all as eccentric as Hoddy, but some could have run him close. *The Irish Times* was not just a national newspaper, it was something of an Irish institution.

So I had no sense at all that I was, in 1968, joining an ailing paper catering mainly for a dwindling minority, and there was certainly no indication of such sentiment inside the office. Its coverage in 1966 of the fiftieth anniversary of the Easter Rising – including much questioning of national, never mind Nationalist myths, notably by Conor Cruise O'Brien – had been an indication of the growing self-confidence of *The Irish Times* in its role as a radical national newspaper, not the mouthpiece of a minority.

In guiding it firmly in this direction Douglas Gageby was, I believe, following his keen instincts as a newspaperman, both editor and manager, rather than his own romantic Nationalism. He must have winced at this paragraph from the Cruiser's *The Embers of Easter* published in April 1966,

> …the Irish State is culturally part of Britain, distinguished from the rest of the archipelago so far mainly by its practice of a puritanical form of the Roman Catholic religion, and by marked deference to ecclesiastical authority.

But Gageby was a more complex man than his breezy, self-assured, no-nonsense demeanour suggested, and a part of him would have agreed with this condemnation of the independent Irish state fifty years after The Rising.

When I met him and began working for him, I knew nothing of his strong political Nationalism, nor of his perceived Fianna Fáil leanings. I assumed that he had joined the *Irish Press* group after the Emergency mainly because he had worked under and got to know Major Vivion De Valera during his days in the Army Intelligence corps, and later, in the Irish News Agency, and, like others in that unit, had been recruited by Vivion. I initially thought that his preference would have been for Fine Gael, given the Army's origins in the pro-Treaty side of the Civil War, and Douglas' great attachment to the Army.

It was only later that I noticed how often he liked to dismiss anyone from Fine Gael, or anyone expressing admiration for that party, as 'an auld Blueshirt', and how he clearly did not share the widespread admiration for Garret FitzGerald when he entered the Dáil and then the Government. It was perhaps the balancing of his editorial instincts and his Fianna Fáil leanings that meant the paper never took any strong party line at election times – even though many, if not most, of the editorial staff in the early seventies were Labour Party supporters and in some cases party members.

Certainly in the many conversations I had with him in those early years, in the office or over lunch, discussing politics, books, the North, badgers, Paris, and paintings, he never challenged my frequent railings against the Southern state in general and Fianna Fáil in particular, nor gave any indication that I was straying on to sensitive territory.

As a comparative newcomer to the paper, I was given a remarkably free rein. As Diplomatic Correspondent I could, more or less, set my own agenda as to where I wanted to travel and write about. Douglas was never mean about expenses, never expected detailed accounting with receipts, and I cannot remember any trip being vetoed because of cost. When I mentioned this to my opposite number on the London *Times* one day as we sat marooned in a distant airport, he looked amazed, and then asked me how he could get a job on *The Irish Times*.

As an editor, Douglas was always open to new ideas. In the run-up to EEC membership he jumped at my suggestion that we should run a weekly 'Europe Page' devoted to news and features on the EEC and other European affairs. Later, I started a 'Developing World' page, to cater similarly for the rapidly growing interest in development aid and Ireland's official and unofficial involvement in it.

Looking back over the files I am surprised at the scope I had for writing comment and analysis on many topics outside my particular remit of foreign and diplomatic affairs. A lot of what I wrote, particularly on Northern Ireland, would not have been to Douglas's personal taste, but almost all of it appeared, albeit, at times, buried at the back of the paper.

Douglas's sudden retirement in July 1974 came as a tremendous shock, but should not really have been a surprise. He had often said that ten years in any job was long enough, and particularly in the job of editor. By 1974 he had been editor of *The Irish Times* for eleven years, and must have been mindful of his own dictum. But I suspect that it was the collapse of the power-sharing Executive in Belfast, barely a month earlier, which pushed him over the edge. That spelled the end of the Sunningdale initiative, and also the eclipse of his own fond hope that a settlement had been found, which could lead to the North, at last, 'coming in'.

The combination of profound disappointment, and personal fatigue after eleven years in a demanding position which was more a way of life than a job, may well have brought him to the sudden realisation that if ten years were enough, eleven were more than enough. As I have said, I do not think he was eased out by the Major because of concern over his Nationalist views on Northern Ireland.

My promotion to Assistant Editor, in the Editor's Office, early in Fergus's tenure meant that I was there sitting opposite Douglas when he returned in 1977, just as suddenly as he had left in 1974. I had stronger feelings, mainly of anger and disappointment, over the manner of Fergus's removal than I had over Douglas's return, though I remember thinking it was not the most imaginative appointment. He himself insisted that his return was just a temporary measure, to see the paper over a difficult period, and he hinted that he would be gone again in two or three years. He was to stay another nine.

Our personal relationship took up where it had left off. There were still the occasional lunches, and I sometimes gave him a lift home at night to his house off Bushy Park Road, which usually meant an invitation in for a nightcap or a cup of coffee with himself and Dorothy. Our differences over Northern policy became more marked, and his resort to dismissing me as a 'tin chapel man' when I put my spoke in at editorial conferences, became more frequent. It was meant to annoy me, but it did not bother me at all. Today it would merit a case before some equality commission.

Every now and again he would present me with some small gift – a print of an old map of Dublin, a book, a sketch map of the Battle of Saintfield, and, much to my delight, two rare volumes of the Belfast journal, *Lagan*, published in 1944 and 1945, and inscribed with the date, 18 June 1982, one 'To Dennis Kennedy; Ulster for Ever. DG' and the other 'To Dennis

Kennedy; Basalt on basalt. DG'. I have always assumed that last was both a compliment and a quotation from somewhere, but I have never been able to trace it.

We never fell out, but from about that point on, our relations were somewhat strained. One bone of contention was promotion in the paper. At the level of Assistant Editor and above, this was entirely at the discretion of Douglas and the Major, and the bases for it were not always apparent. Titles, such as Assistant or Deputy Editor, did not always imply any change of function or additional responsibility, but they did bring a higher salary and other perks of office. I was conspicuously omitted from one or two such rounds of promotions in the early 1980s, and complained to Douglas. He muttered some excuses, and said he would have a word with Tom, Tom being the Major. Within a month or so I had a company car, no small perk if you lived in Glencullen, and, in 1982, I found myself a Deputy Editor.

One reason for my being passed over may have been the fact that I had enrolled at Trinity for a PhD, working at it part time and hoping to complete it within four years. I was dividing my time between *The Irish Times* office, Trinity, and the National Library. Douglas was not too keen on this, and seemed to assume that I was losing interest in journalism and looking towards an academic career. In this he was mistaken.

The idea of returning to study at post-graduate level, albeit part-time, had first struck me one lazy summer morning at the news desk in the late seventies. Donal Foley, trawling through that day's paper, turned to me and said, 'What I don't understand, Dennis, is why John Taylor hates the Irish language so much?'

I tried to explain to Donal that it was not so much the language itself that annoyed the fiery Unionist Taylor, but that the iconic place afforded it in the Republic was one of the handiest clubs he could find for berating the hypocrisy and folly of Irish Nationalism. That conversation set me thinking about how little even intelligent and generous men like Donal understood Northern attitudes towards the South. A year later I had enrolled at Trinity for a PhD on the rather unwieldy topic of Northern Attitudes to the Independent Irish State, 1919–1949.

For some time I had been more and more aware of what I called the amateur status of journalists. As a specialist correspondent on the EEC and on Irish foreign policy, I was invited to chair discussions at seminars, and to speak on topics such as Irish neutrality, almost always in the company of professional diplomats and highly qualified academics. I usually protested that a journalist was, by definition, not an expert on such topics; he might be an expert at communicating them, but his knowledge could rarely be more than superficial, as his job did not allow time for extensive research, or for long deliberation.

The more I said this, the more frustrated I was at knowing a bit about a lot of things, but never being really expert on one chosen area. One fellow labourer on the seminar circuit, Patrick Keating of Trinity, with whom I discussed these thoughts, encouraged me to sign up for a PhD, which I did, with Patrick as my supervisor. I spent the next four years – actually it was more like five – happily combining research with journalism.

This was not as difficult as it sounds, for by then Dublin journalists were mostly on a four-day week, a bonus negotiated to compensate for the unsocial hours we had to work. I was usually doing three nights a week in the editor's chair, which entailed starting at about five in the afternoon and working at least until the first edition went to print around midnight, and usually a while after that. I soon established a routine of going into the National Library at ten in the morning, and working through to five – with a cup of coffee and a tomato sandwich in Bushwell's for lunch, before heading down to Fleet Street. I also had three full days off work each week, so I was, certainly for the last two years of work on my thesis, able to combine full-time study with full-time work.

My television-viewing suffered a bit, as did our theatre and cinema going, and I never did get round to finishing the bits and pieces of building on 'Whin Cottage' which I had been meaning to tackle since 1971. But the thesis was finished by 1984, the final scramble being facilitated by the five-week sabbatical leave I was granted under a new scheme I had helped bring in in my final role as Deputy Editor (Administration). Five weeks was the maximum allowed.

Being Deputy Editor took me out of the editor's office and into more frequent trips down to the Bunker to see the Major. It also took me, to a considerable extent, away from writing and reporting. I suspected that Douglas's motivation in giving me that particular job might have been, in part at least, to stop me peddling my heresies on the North and allied policies in the pages of the paper. That may be unduly cynical; it might have been a trial to see how well I could handle budgets, logistics and personnel, in other words to see if I had the makings of an editor in me.

That was how the Major's mind worked, and by that time there was already speculation about when Douglas would finally retire, and who would succeed him. In 1984 he had been back for seven years, not the two or three he had originally indicated. It was fairly certain there would be an internal appointment, and the three names emerging in the news room gossip were Jim Downey, Conor Brady and myself. Jim and I were already Deputy Editors, and Conor soon became one. We were the most senior people in the paper who were still young enough to be considered for the appointment.

I was fairly certain I had no chance. I knew Douglas would do all he could to block me, not just because we disagreed strongly over policy on Northern Ireland, but because he may well have thought that any radical change of approach on that issue could have been commercially damaging for the paper. I was aware, from the regular conversations I now had with the Major, that his views on Northern Ireland were closer to mine than to Douglas's – he made it clear that he hoped that I would be a restraining influence on Douglas.

But the Major was essentially cautious, and I concluded that he would, in the event, agree with Douglas that making me editor would be far too big a gamble. That is assuming that, leaving aside Northern Ireland, they would have thought me up to the job, which was something I could not assume.

That left me with a dilemma. I knew Jim and Conor very well, and had worked closely with both of them for considerable periods, Conor, in fact, had been my assistant on the new Europe page in his early days with *The Irish Times*. I was on excellent terms with them, but I did not relish the thought of spending the rest of my career working under either of them.

Jim had long experience and supreme self-confidence, but we were very different people, and I had no doubt working for him would be far more difficult than working with him.

Conor was much younger, but had had wider experience, including that of editing a national newspaper. He was far less political than Jim, indeed was hardly political at all. Moreover he had already joined and left *The Irish Times*, rejoined and left again, and come close to doing it a third time. I sometimes thought his mind seemed to be more on the next job, rather than his present one. I feared our warm friendship would not survive long with him in the chair.

Then, out of the blue, in 1985, came a suggestion I could not dismiss. Sitting in the bar of the European Parliament in Strasbourg early that year

I was approached by a friend not without influence in the corridors of Europe. Did I know that the job of European Commission representative in Northern Ireland was about to become vacant, and would I be interested in it? If I was, he thought I had a good chance of getting it, and he would do what he could to back me. I should think about it.

I did, and realised that this could be an escape route from an *Irish Times* under either Jim or Conor, into an area where I would have some expertise, a high salary and be boss of my own tiny domain in Belfast. That was the downside, it would be in Belfast, to which I had promised myself I would never return. But then again it would be an appointment on a short contract, four years at the most.

But would I fit into a bureaucracy like the Commission? I found out more about the job, and was comforted to know that its main function was information. Instead of writing pithy articles explaining the workings of the European Community to readers of *The Irish Times*, I would be writing pithy press releases on the same subjects, and delivering stimulating addresses to Farmers Unions, Rotary Clubs and local councils.

Early days in Glencullen; three-year old Diarmuid Kennedy among the buttercups in meadow in front of 'Whin Cottage'.

Then I discovered there would be strong competition for the post: a professional economist, a front-line politician, and a prominent civil servant were among the likely applicants. I was told I would need to canvass hard if I was to have a chance. Canvass where and whom? The MEPs, of course. That meant Ian Paisley, John Taylor and John Hume. Paisley I had long regarded as the devil incarnate, John Taylor and I had been sworn enemies since our days together at Queen's, and I had written dozens of articles criticising John Hume.

So I decided to canvass no one, and simply take my luck with an application, even though I was sure I had little chance against the other strong candidates. I applied, was short-listed and interviewed in Belfast. I then went off on a long-planned holiday with Katherine and our younger son to Sweden. There we spent the most of July 1985 in a holiday 'willage' in the middle of Vastergotland, cut off from the rest of the world, before embarking on a leisurely drive home, via ferry from Gothenburg to Tyneside, and across the north of England. Just before embarking on the boat at Holyhead I phoned our older son Diarmuid, who had been at home in 'Whin Cottage'.

'Where on earth have you been? Everyone is looking for you – the papers, Brussels, London, they've all been on wanting to know where you are.'

A mix-up in the London office of the Commission had, it seemed, resulted in a premature announcement of the decision to offer me the Belfast job. This had provoked such a furious reaction from Paisley, Taylor and others, that the Commission had no option but to confirm the news and say I had been appointed. That was why they had been so anxious to contact me. In fact I was never offered the job, but simply accepted the appointment which had already been made.

Paisley denounced me as a Republican, and a Dublin plant. Taylor vowed he would never set foot in the Belfast office so long as I was there. (He kept his word, though we talked often enough on the telephone.) The UDA, or its like, sent me a live bullet by post to 'Whin Cottage', with a scrawled note indicating they had another one waiting for me. Within a month, I was out of *The Irish Times* and on the train to Belfast. Within sixteen months Douglas was out and Conor Brady was editor.

The photographs of my farewell in the newsroom in August 1985 show a broadly smiling Douglas Gageby, and a rather rueful-looking Dennis Kennedy. I think Douglas was happier to be rid of me than I was to leave. I loved working for *The Irish Times*; I still read it every day, though much of its content has little relevance to a reader in Northern Ireland. Once I left the European Commission I started submitting the odd article as a means of relieving my own blood pressure, and probably heightening that of some *Irish Times* readers.

Even back in the seventies *The Irish Times* was being spoken of as a great newspaper; now it is often described as one of the world's great newspapers. It is not, and never was; no paper produced in Dublin with the slender resources available to any Irish paper could hope to be classed as one of the great newspapers of the world. But it was a very good newspaper, the best on the island, and played an important role in the modernisation of Irish society, particularly in the late sixties and seventies. Above all else it had its own style; it was unique.

Was Douglas Gageby a great editor? He was certainly a very good one, and would probably have dismissed the question of whether or not he was a great one as irrelevant, as stuff and nonsense. He was also a lucky one; he first took control of the paper in the sixties, at a time when Irish society, more prosperous than hitherto, more open in its thinking, needed just the sort of journalism the revitalised *Irish Times* was offering; he was lucky in 1974, getting out just as the oil crisis was beginning to hit the newspaper industry; and he was lucky again in 1977, coming back when the economic upturn was about to throw a life-line to ailing papers.

He was undoubtedly an outstandingly successful editor in the commercial sense, and though luck may have played a part in that, he had a wonderful knack of knowing what would, or would not, work in selling the paper. He was ahead of the pack in deciding to give half a page to TV and radio programmes at a time when the paper was bursting with both news and advertising, and competition for space was fierce. Why should we give half a page of free publicity to our competitors, some of us argued. But he went ahead and did it, and soon, so did everyone else, except by then it was full page.

He was an unusual editor in that he was never a public figure, never a leading participant in public debate or even public life, despite being editor of the country's foremost newspaper for two decades. Nor was he a writing editor. He did write many editorials, but almost nothing else. His editorials were good, but not memorable – at least I cannot remember any he wrote in my time, and when Andrew Whittaker, in 2007, produced his *Bright Brilliant Days* book of essays in praise of Gageby, while many contributors sang the praises of Douglas's editorials in general, no one cited a specific instance. The only writing actually by him included in that book is a series of articles

Goodbye to *The Irish Times*. August 1985, Douglas Gageby says farewell to the author. (Photo *The Irish Times*)

on Germany, written for the *Irish Press* in 1946.

But he could write very well. One editorial, written before my time but quoted to me by Donal Foley in my early days in the paper, beautifully encapsulates both his style and the more engaging aspects of his personality. He wrote it at the time of the Bishop and the Nightie Controversy which rocked the nation in 1966 after a guest on the RTE's flagship 'Late Late Show' admitted to Gay Byrne that she had worn, not a nightie, but nothing at all on the first night of her honeymoon. This provoked ringing denunciations of the poor bride, the programme, the host Gay Byrne, RTE and even the Government, from several outraged members of the Catholic Hierarchy. After the uproar had lasted for a week, Gageby penned an editorial beginning, 'The country is going to hell, but the bishops are on to it'. His most damming criticism of any person or piece of writing was that he, or it, was 'po-faced'. Under him *The Irish Times* was never po-faced, or hardly ever.

One piece of writing he must surely have regretted almost as soon as it appeared. In April 1984, Russell Murphy, one of Dublin's leading account-ants, *bon viveur* and patron of the arts, died suddenly. He had been accountant, advisor and friend to the rich and famous, the great and the good, including, it was rumoured, Douglas Gageby. Almost immediately, and most uncharacteristically, Douglas published an appreciation, over his own initials. The praise was extravagant; the deceased was described as an accountant and financial adviser 'of impeccable integrity and standing ... who cut no corners and allowed none of his clients to do so.' It was an unrestrained eulogy of Murphy, both as an accountant, and as a man. It concluded with an unmistakably Gagebyesque five-word sentence: 'There is a great gap.'

Unfortunately it soon emerged that there was indeed a great gap, but it was between the money his clients had entrusted to Mr Murphy, and the amounts still there when the books were opened. Gay Byrne, Hugh Leonard and other luminaries found themselves considerably out of pocket, as, according to the gleeful gossip around the newsroom, did Douglas Gageby. That cheered us all up, as the story in general did most of Dublin.

One downside to an otherwise genial personality was Douglas's tendency to take against individuals, public figures as well as colleagues, and to consign them permanently to categories defined in barrack-room language. Once an individual was designated a s**t, he was a s**t forever, and his views did not merit consideration.

An editor has to be judged not just on how well he ran his newspaper, nor how successfully, nor on how well he wrote, but on the impact the paper, under him, had on the community it was serving and the problems it was facing. On many counts Douglas Gageby scores highly on this. The paper, certainly in his first period of editorship, was in the vanguard of the sort of social change the country needed; it was central in the questioning of the founding myths of the state, as in 1966 and in articles it carried in the early days of the Troubles, even though many of these may not have reflected his own personal views.

But he was not a political radical. His great interest in the North, and his determination to maximise *Irish Times* coverage of it, was intended to shake the South out of its apathy on the North. It was not meant to challenge traditional Nationalist attitudes. His hero in the SDLP, which he greatly admired, was John Hume, not Gerry Fitt or Paddy Devlin, though he was on good terms with Devlin, a frequent visitor to the office.

He was not radical in terms of Southern politics. His loyalty to John Healy over the years, despite much opposition to Healy among the staff, was in part personal, but also probably driven by a desire to balance the more liberal, radical, contributions from Michael MacInerney, Conor Cruise O'Brien, and later, Dick Walsh. His acute commercial sense may have played a part too; Healy chronicled, and glamorised, the coarse and the cynical in Irish political life, elements which were, and maybe still are, more prevalent than the high-minded and principled, and in so doing attracted and held a readership for the paper which might have had little taste for its more liberal content.

But there were many in the office who believed that the paper could have done more under his editorship to attack the self-serving, complacent politics and politicians of that era, and some who felt strongly that it was far too tolerant of Charles Haughey and the corruption he personified.

For me it was on the North, the subject he felt most passionate about, that he was most misguided. His hatred of Unionism and Unionists was irrational, and a serious flaw in an editor of *The Irish Times* at such a critical period. His self-confessed romantic Nationalism was a handicap at a time crying out for a fundamental re-examination of Nationalism as a force in Irish politics. At one level he was the great scourge of Irish humbug, and that was reflected in much of the paper's content in the late sixties and seventies. But he could never bring himself to see that the greatest humbug of all was arguably the rhetorical Nationalism of the politicians, and its potential, at critical times, to envelop almost the entire country, including *The Irish Times,* in a green haze thick enough to smother rational debate.

It is still greatly to his credit, as an editor, that he brought in Conor Cruise O'Brien as a columnist in the early eighties, even though he disagreed fundamentally with him, and indeed detested much of what he wrote. But it is also to his discredit that he lost Conor at a crucial time: just after the Anglo-Irish Agreement, and just before he himself relinquished the editorship. I believe Conor could have been persuaded to stay with *The Irish Times,* and should have been.

Douglas's best period was undoubtedly his first term as editor. When he came back in 1977 his priority was the commercial welfare of the paper. He devoted his energy to boosting sales, to promotional campaigns as a means of doing so rather, perhaps, than concentrating on improving the quality of the paper and preserving its unique character. He was also, I think, depressed at the continuing violence in the North. When the Government, first under Haughey and later FitzGerald, pursued an essentially Nationalist agenda linked to close cooperation with London, as in the New Ireland Forum and the Anglo-Irish Agreement, the *Irish Times* went along with it; it became part of a green consensus, when, of all Southern papers, it should have been uniquely qualified to challenge it.

Even before his departure the paper was beginning to lose some of its distinct personality. After it, this was more marked, and *The Irish Times* moved, as in the title of Dermot James' 2007 book, from the margins to the centre. Instead of being off-centre radical, it joined the establishment, and became, with prosperity, like that establishment: increasingly self-satisfied, self-centred and somewhat unthinking.

But not entirely. It is still a good paper, with flashes of eccentricity and originality, though it is sad to see it leaving itself open to the sneers and jibes of those who would once have given their right hands to be allowed into its pages.

Twenty-One

You Don't Understand

'You don't understand, Dennis,' said my journalist friend Raymond Smith to me one morning in Boston, in the mid-1970s, after a press breakfast where Garret FitzGerald had been briefing American journalists on all matters Irish. Raymond was putting me straight on how Irish journalists behave abroad. 'You're still fairly new, but you have to understand that when we are abroad, we all stick together. We journalists and everybody else. We don't contradict each other. That's letting the side down.'

At the briefing there had been some questions on the need for social reform in Ireland, about the laws on the sale of contraceptives, which Garret had dealt with. Then someone asked about abortion. It was illegal, said Garret, and no one in Ireland wanted to legalise it. It was not an issue. At which point I politely suggested it was, and mentioned the hundreds of Irish women travelling each year to Great Britain to have terminations, plus the small groups who were trying to raise awareness of the problem in Ireland.

'You don't understand, Dennis,' said Commissioner Patrick Hillery to me one day at lunch in the Westbury Hotel in Brussels. It was November 1976, and he had just been called out of the room to take a phone call from Dublin. On his return he told us, three or four journalists and some of his officials, that that had been Jack (Lynch) on the phone, and he wanted Hillery to let himself be nominated for the Presidency, after the sudden resignation of President O'Dalaigh.

In the burst of conversation that followed I told him I thought he would be mad to accept. He was almost four years into the new world of the European Community, and was enjoying it. Seven years in the Park was a life sentence as far as his career was concerned. He smiled at me and said 'You don't understand, Dennis. When someone asks you to be President of Ireland, you can't refuse.'

'But you couldn't understand, Dennis, being from the North,' said Micheal O Loinsigh, as he and his colleagues from the Irish Sovereignty Movement sat in the editor's office in the run-up to the 1972 referendum. They had come to complain to Gageby about our coverage of the campaign, and he had asked me to sit in with him. What I could not understand, 'being from the North', was some point about Irish sovereignty.

The first two instances at least were friendly words of advice, from people I knew well and liked. But looking back, they neatly sum up a widespread attitude towards Northern Protestants like me who had decided to make their home in the Republic. What it was I did not, or could not, understand was the very narrow concept of Irishness that had emerged during the long struggle for independence, and had solidified during the claustrophobic years since the foundation of the state. My problem, though in fact it was their problem, was that I was not a member of their tribe.

Despite the constant rhetoric of one island, of Catholic, Protestant and dissenter, the Irishness embodied in the state was Catholic, Gaelic and intensely Nationalistic. I was from Co. Antrim, which most people in the Republic had never visited, I was Protestant, I did not speak Irish, nor even pretend to, I played hockey not hurling, I was not a rabid Nationalist. Had I be able to tick even one of the right boxes, I would have been a member of the tribe. But I did not, and though I was personally very welcome, I could not really be expected to understand things Irish.

Yet I had come to Dublin with an Irish passport, with no doubt at all about my Irish identity, with the vague hope that sometime in the future I, or my children, might be living in a united island. I had come cheerfully confident that all the people on the island were Irish, that I was as Irish as a Gaelghoir from Galway, a Catholic from Cork or an atheist from Athlone. I had read The Proclamation and knew that the sacred text of the state guaranteed me religious and civil liberty, and promised to cherish me equally.

I was not so naïve as to believe that these theoretical truths bore any close relationship to reality in the Wholly Catholic Republic, but I had no doubt that my concept of Irishness was the right one, and it was Ray, Paddy and Micheal who did not understand. Perhaps I saw it as my task to help them see the light. I was, after all, just back from a couple of years as a missionary in Africa.

When I was asked, as I repeatedly was by friends and relatives in the North, and by other visitors to Dublin, if I had any difficulty identifying with the state in which I lived, or with my fellow Southerners, I said not at all, but they had some difficulty identifying with me. That was a wry comment rather than a criticism. I was well used to being in a minority, having been a non-conformist from my childhood, not just in religion.

But in the Ireland of the early seventies I felt part of a vigorous, growing and, at the time, seemingly unstoppable minority – a liberal, reforming minority that was challenging the Constitution and its outmoded assertions on Northern Ireland, divorce, and the special place of the Catholic Church, was demanding change in the laws on the Irish language, censorship and the import and sale of contraceptives, was calling for reform in the whole education system, and was even suggesting the nation might be spared the twice daily Angelus on RTE.

This minority in the early seventies, if anyone had paused to think about such things, was neither Northern nor Protestant, but almost entirely mainstream Southern Catholic. It was not one movement, but across the spectrum of Irish society a variety of individuals and groups who were challenging different elements of conventional Irishness – Mary Robinson and John Horgan on contraception, Conor Cruise O'Brien on the myths of Nationalism, the Language Freedom Movement on the Irish language. Even the defenders of Georgian Dublin against the rampaging developers were, in part, confronting a chauvinistic mindset that saw nothing from British times as worth preserving.

So I never felt excluded, or an outsider. Rather I was very much in tune with what we thought was a liberal tide which was going to change Ireland for the better, and *The Irish Times* was right at the centre of it. For me joining the European Economic Community promised to be the historic watershed between the old, inward-looking, isolated Nationalist Ireland, and the new, liberal modern one.

Nor was my life in Dublin one of endless confrontation. I was very happy, I loved working for *The Irish Times*, I loved Dublin, and I loved exploring more and more of the island. We had an ever-widening and very mixed circle of friends, some from *The Irish Times* and journalism generally, some from 'the Department', some from foreign embassies, some from Kilternan parish, some from Methodism and some who dated back to Katherine's or my former existences in Dublin or the North.

Our friends and neighbours in Glencullen were little bothered about identity – theirs or ours. We talked, rather, about the deafening noise from the new water-jet contraption the quarry had installed to cut granite, or the pollution of the Glencullen river by the effluent, or the way people from Foxrock drove up to Glencullen to dump their rubbish, or the problems of getting planning permission – and of building without it – or of the new Frauchan Festival that was drawing crowds to a marquee near the pub every July.

The only thing I wrote for *The Irish Times* which excited much local interest was a short note on the delights of the 44B bus which I contributed to a series on daily outings. One local cut it out and had it framed.

Life in Glencullen was great, and all around, in politics, in the economy, in *The Irish Times,* things were looking up.

The high point of my optimism as a new immigrant to the fair republic was the EEC referendum of May 1972. The year, the bloodiest of all the Troubles, had begun appallingly with Bloody Sunday in Derry followed by the burning of the British Embassy in Dublin. Yet within days, both Ireland and the United Kingdom had signed the Treaty that would bind them together as members of the European Economic Community.

The long and heated debate on the referendum to ratify that treaty seemed to me to reflect that same clash of past with future symbolised by the burning of the embassy of one signatory by a tribal mob in the capital of the other, on the eve of both countries signing up for membership of a European Community designed to consign the worst manifestations of Nationalism to the past.

The most vigorous opposition to membership was strongly Nationalistic. Republican groups played a key role in the 'no' camp. Joining the EEC alongside Britain would be selling out the ideal of Irish unification; Irish neutrality would end; all sorts of wickedness and continental immorality would infect Irish purity. As a specialist journalist on the EEC, I had a busy time, and as well as writing a great deal, I was sometimes invited to speak at public meetings, not as an advocate of a Yes or No but as someone with expert knowledge on the subject.

One night in a room in Ballina packed with about 200 people, I was on a panel alongside Mary Robinson and several others, and was sufficiently moved to forget my supposed neutrality. Late in the evening a local priest, prominent in the No campaign, delivered an impassioned address from the back of the hall. He listed all the above threats, plus many more, and concluded by saying that membership of the EEC would most certainly mean the destruction of the Irish way of life. The chairman asked me to respond. I could not help myself – I told the meeting that having listened to Father X's detailed description of what he clearly saw as the Irish way of life, I thought the promise of its destruction was the most convincing argument I had yet heard for voting yes.

As the May voting date approached it was clear that the Government was worried about the outcome. The worsening situation in Northern Ireland, the evident strength of the IRA, and widespread concern in the Republic for the safety of Northern Catholics were all having an effect on public opinion, the impact of which on the referendum vote was difficult to predict.

When the referendum was approved by a five to one majority, on a high poll, I thought it was much more than a vote for the EEC. I convinced myself that it was a vote against crude Nationalism, and above all that it was a clear rejection of the use of violence for political ends. An added boost to optimism came in a further referendum in December 1972, when the people voted to end the State's recognition of 'the special position of the Holy Catholic, Apostolic and Roman Church'.

When, to widespread surprise, a Fine Gael–Labour coalition defeated Fianna Fáil in a general election and came to power early in 1973, things seemed even better. The seventies might not, after all, be Socialist, but they were looking pretty good, even in Northern Ireland. There the British Government proposals in March of that year for a power-sharing executive had survived an Assembly election in June, and stuttering progress was made towards an Agreement, actually achieved at Sunningdale in December.

But it was not to be. My optimism had begun to wane when I saw a Council of Ireland was included in the Sunningdale Agreement, for I was sure Brian Faulkner could not sell it to the Unionist voters. It sunk even lower when, on a visit to my home town of Lisburn, I saw the masked thugs of the UDA strutting around the town with their pick-age handles. The Ulster Workers Strike helped ensure that the Executive collapsed.

But it was not just the North that was looking somewhat less promising. In the South the oil crisis plunged us all in gloom, especially those of us living in Glencullen and heavily dependent on petrol. Even under a coalition government the pace of reform was not what I had hoped for, and a rather silly brand of Nationalism still seemed alive and well.

In 1978 I wrote an article in *The Irish Times* headed 'Ten years in the nettle country of the Republic'. The reference was to a Jack Lynch speech of the early seventies in which he had declared that 'nettles had to be grasped' as regards the North and related issues. The real disappointment of the decade, I wrote, was that no nettles had been grasped, and that the cultural revolution that looked like beginning in the early seventies had lost its momentum.

Thinking on the North has returned to simplicities like the inevitability of unification, or the logic of geography. Appreciation of the variety of northern Protestant attitudes and what prompts them has been lost, in some cases engulfed in a wave of sentimentality about the North that sees it as an Eden, the population of which have hearts of gold, are rocks of common sense, and will, shortly, see the green light.

It is as if the South, collectively, had made an intellectual effort to understand the North, to sympathise with the fears, doubts and even prejudices of the people there, and had tried to find solutions, but that failure, particularly of Sunningdale, has in time led to an intellectual exhaustion and a return to the easy option of simplistic nationalism – all inherent in the attitude that sees British withdrawal as the key to progress.

In June 1981, in another article entitled 'Wholly Catholic Ireland' I wrote that, for a Northerner living in the Republic, the general election of that month was 'profoundly depressing'. The two reasons I gave were the apparent backing all three major parties had given to the insertion of a ban on abortion into the Constitution, and what I called a closing of Nationalist minds on the H-Blocks issue (The hunger strike at the Maze had just been called off after the death of ten prisoners.)

My argument was not that abortion should be legalised (though I would have supported such a move) but that a Constitutional ban on the legislature ever doing so was to raise the issue to a level above political debate, enshrining in the Constitution an essentially Catholic viewpoint, and implying that anyone not accepting Catholic teaching on abortion was somehow 'unIrish'. On the H-Blocks I pointed out that the three parties had rejected the IRA prisoners' demand for political status, but were at the same time demanding 'flexibilty' from Mrs Thatcher in her handling of that very issue.

The H-Blocks had helped raise the Nationalist temperature in the South, and though the Haughey-led Fianna Fáil government's policy on the North was unity by consent, it was at the same time demanding a formal commitment from London to Irish unity, whether or not the North had consented; this, I wrote, was hypocrisy. The political scene, I concluded, was beginning to look like a Catholic and Nationalist wilderness, badly in need of a wind of change.

It was clear by then that the historic vote of May 1972 had not been the watershed I had hoped, and that, in some ways, the South had become more Nationalistic, not less, or perhaps a new type of Nationalism was emerging. Ironically, one of the places I noticed this was where I expected it least: among the Irish in Brussels. After 1973 a substantial Irish community grew up around the European Commission and other European institutions, made up of officials, diplomats and representatives of various commercial and promotional bodies. A considerable number of these I had come to know during the negotiations for entry, and some had become close personal friends. These expatriates included people of high ability and dedication, plus the inevitable quota of placemen and chancers.

They may have gone to Brussels with the uncertainties of new boys, in some cases patronised by their British counterparts, but they rapidly overcame any such complexes, proved themselves able and, in general, did very well. They also became very popular, partly because Ireland and the Irish were soon seen as 'good' Europeans, in stark contrast to the British who were, from their earliest days, turning out to be extremely awkward customers. I think it was the Irish in Brussels who first popularised the term 'the Brits' to describe their fellow Europeans from the United Kingdom. The label sounded, to me, dismissive, even arrogant. A cheerful happiness in being Irish was turning into an overweening pride and conceit.

As the seventies became the eighties, the chauvinism of many of the Brussels Irish, particularly as regards the British, became more evident, and displayed itself increasingly in discussion of Northern Ireland. My conversations in Brussels became more heated. In Dublin the same lurch towards the green end of the spectrum could also be seen, probably the result, in part, of the influence of the Haughey-led Fianna Fáil. It was happening in the Department of Foreign Affairs, within which I still had many friends. Encouraged perhaps by Haughey's interference in the Department, a distinction was developing between 'true believers' – the phrase used privately in house to describe those officials perceived as Haughey supporters and advocates of a more Nationalistic line on Northern Ireland – and others who saw themselves as professional diplomats implementing policy, and a small minority who seriously questioned the green line.

The New Ireland Forum of the main Nationalist parties on the island produced a report in 1984 which is still hailed as a step forward, a generous and flexible reformulation of Nationalism. But it was, fundamentally, a restatement of traditional Nationalist claims, placing blame for partition on London, and accusing Unionists of systematically denying basic rights to the minority community. It was an assertive Nationalism that was to characterise Dublin's partisan approach to the Northern problem, and confuse the issue for long after I left the Republic.

One of the ironies of Ireland in more recent times, particularly in the era of the Celtic Tiger, has been that the great majority of the people, in their daily lives, have moved further and further away from the household gods of Irish Nationalist identity – Catholicism, the Irish language, the pursuit of unification – but have, at the same time, developed what might be called a secular Nationalism. The state and the body politic have been much slower to do so. Politicians still put unification at the top of their agendas, or at least of their rhetoric, push the language, rush to celebrate the violent Republicanism of 1916 to 1921, and still feel they have to keep Britain and things British (including Queen Elizabeth II) at arms length. And the mournful Angelus still rings on RTE.

All the while, in the country at large, an alternative secular Nationalism has been flourishing – it is not assertively Catholic, or Catholic at all, nor Gaelic, and cares very little about the North and unification. But it became self consciously, even arrogantly Irish to an alarming degree, and was seen at its most unbecoming on the 'No' side in successive referendum campaigns on Europe, where some of the most articulate critics of the old Nationalism succumbed to the new and trumpeted their concern for national veto, voice and sovereignty.

But even the early indications of this trend had nothing to do with my rather sudden exodus from the Republic in 1985. It was entirely circumstantial; I was offered an extremely attractive post representing the European Commission in Belfast on a four-year contract, and I intended to return to Dublin at the end of it. My two older children were at university in Dublin, and 'Whin Cottage' continued to be their home, and mine at weekends and holidays. In the event, the contract was extended to six, and a return to Dublin was problematic. Then the Celtic Tiger, by sending the cost of living through the roof, priced me out of the market.

In the two decades that I lived and worked in the Republic I was often critical of aspects of its politics and society. That is the proper function of a journalist. But we were very happy there, and never thought we would leave, and certainly never contemplated returning to Northern Ireland. While the sectarian division in the North became steadily worse and elements on each side went to war with each other, and thousands died, we lived in peace and harmony with our Southern Catholic neighbours.

The instances of any resentment or abuse encountered by us, or related to us, are noteworthy only because of their extreme rarity. Our children were on one occasion crudely told to go back where they came from by a neighbour after some local altercation, and were at times jeeringly called Black Protestants, or Black Northerners by other children. When they went to Wesley College they were ostracised on the Glencullen bus, but probably as much on grounds of social difference or inter-school rivalry as religion or perceived origins. Our garage door was stoned a few times, but maybe out of devilment, or resentment at blow-ins.

We did meet one young Protestant supply teacher who told us the hayshed at her family farm down the country had been burned down after Bloody Sunday, and another friend had first hand experience of boys at a Protestant boarding school in Donegal being terrorised by local youths. I was begged not to write about these incidents in *The Irish Times* as that might make things worse. Perhaps more worrying, the genteel lady who called round to selected houses in Glencullen every autumn to sell Remembrance Day poppies and raise funds for the British Legion, suddenly stopped calling. She had been warned off, told not to come back to Glencullen with her poppies.

But that was all – the sum total of unpleasantness visited on us over two decades living in Dublin, while 3,000 people were dying violent deaths a hundred miles to the north.

At times in the peace and quiet of Glencullen, we seemed isolated from and insulated against all that. We knew that the husband of one of our neighbours had been in jail for 'Republican' activities, and had absconded while on bail in connection with another similar offence, but the wife was both a helpful neighbour and, in time, a good friend. When we were approached by a lady from Kilternan Church of Ireland in 1972 and asked if we thought they should start gathering blankets and other supplies for Protestant refugees who might have to flee their homes in Belfast, we were amazed and even amused.

But in other ways Northern Ireland was far from remote. In addition to my fairly regular journalistic forays North, we went frequently to visit my family – my parents, my brother, my sister-in-law, and their three children were living in Lisburn – and to see the Giant's Causeway and the Mountains of Mourne, and to climb my own sacred peak, Slemish in Co. Antrim. My relatives came to stay in Glencullen.

My father, who was working in a chemist's shop in the Ardoyne district of Belfast had survived one IRA attack, when a gang of young terrorists had been beaten off with a fusillade of tins of baby food. The local IRA command subsequently apologised. But a second raid saw the shop badly damaged by a firebomb, and when a third attack totally destroyed it, the owner said that was enough, and the shop was out of business and my father, in his sixties, out of a job. But that was small price compared to what other families had to pay. No one in our whole family connection was injured in the Troubles, let alone killed.

Besides family, I still had many friends in the North, and made a point of seeing some of them on each visit. This kept me in touch with old journalistic colleagues, and, in particular, with some Catholic friends who could give me their close-up perspective on the worst of the violence in Belfast. They, in turn, became regular visitors at 'Whin Cottage'.

As I write this the politicians are celebrating the tenth anniversary of the Belfast Agreement, and congratulating each other on bringing peace to Ireland. I am not at all sure an uncertain peace which puts in power those who caused so much of the death, division and bitterness is something to be celebrated. It might be more appropriate to ponder quietly how on earth the politicians, two governments, churchmen, commentators and all the rest of us, let a minor territorial dispute and too-well-nurtured historical grievances turn into a nightmare of terrorist violence and communal strife that raged for thirty years in twentieth-century western Europe.

The state where I lived and worked for the worst of that period has to share the blame. To enshrine as its great heroes men who resorted to dreadful violence to achieve political ends, is to keep rich the soil for new violent harvests. Successive governments in Dublin denounced the Provisional IRA and the resort to terrorism, but did they do all that could, and should have done to deny any base or succour to the terrorists? Did the subsequent rush to do a deal with the terrorists, to make concession after concession to an organisation which was illegal, and was itself a threat to the state, suggest that there was, all along, a fatal ambivalence towards the men of violence?

The violence took more than 3,000 lives, and devastated the economy of Northern Ireland, denying it three decades of growth and development. Towns all over the province were repeatedly bombed. The Republic suffered devastating attacks in Dublin and Monaghan, and paid a heavy economic price for security. But all this was on foot of a quarrel which, as John Hume kept saying, was never worth a single life. It should never have been allowed to happen.

Northern Ireland, as a place apart, is hard to take. I first left it in the 1960s because I felt I had to escape from its suffocating smugness and provincialism. Viewing it from a Southern perspective during the Troubles my family – mainly my children – dubbed it Our Wee Province (OWP for short) in mockery of the enormously inflated regard its people seemed to have for every aspect of life there, past and present. Understandable pride in the biggest shipyard/rope works/spinning mill in the world had been replaced by a perverse pride in having the worst Troubles and the most appalling terrorists. Even today, in a period of welcome if precarious peace, its icons remain a ship that sank on its first voyage, and a footballer who drank himself to an early grave. There is public rejoicing over each new soulless shopping centre.

Its parts are better than the whole; Slemish remains a magic mountain and the Antrim coast and glens look serenely beautiful. So do the Mournes and the Fermanagh lakes. Perhaps Douglas Gageby had something when he insisted that the two parts of Ireland needed each other; as separate, they left much to be desired.

One day in June 2007, while staying in Dublin, Katherine and I, on a whim, drove up to Glencullen. Neither of us had been back for several years, and it was fifteen years since we had sold 'Whin Cottage'. We were unsure of what we would find, and whether we were wise to return. But the sun was shining and the only sounds we could hear as we walked down Barrack Road past where Mr Manning had anchored his van, were the birds singing and the tap tap of a stone cutter at work. The valley stretched gloriously away to the distant Sugar Loaf on our left, and ahead to the great wall of Glencullen Mountain.

We looked over the hedge into the garden of 'Whin Cottage', immaculately kept by its new owners. We picked out and listed the trees we had planted, the conifers, mountain ash and weeping birch, and the metasequoia. Any pain we felt at no longer living there or owning the cottage, was considerably eased by the obtrusive presence of a large new house, plonked in Houlihan's field, almost right in front of 'Whin Cottage' and near enough to mar the prospect and spoil the grandeur and romance of the setting.

On our way back towards Fox's totally reinvented pub we saw that the pillars of the Grand Gates of Glencullen House had been tumbled. A few yards on we passed the stone cutter at work, and recognised an old friend. We talked for an hour about Glencullen. He told us Glencullen House was deserted and in a bad way. No one knew what was going to happen to it.[i] Then we went to say goodbye to the Colonel, and to Gertie and Johnny Cotter, and to Ena and John Cotter, and to Jack Flanagan and Mary Parker, to Jack Mulvey, quiet at last, all lying peacefully in the sunshine, in the well-tended graveyard behind the church, the Two Rock up behind it and ahead the hazy vista across to the Sugar Loaf.

Glencullen seemed the most beautiful spot on earth. Happy days.

(i). After our visit Glencullen House was again sold, and restoration work on it began in 2008.

Postscript

I came to Dublin in 1968 buoyed in part, as I have written, by a pleasant romantic Nationalism. I would probably, if pressed, have called myself a Nationalist. Would I still have done so when I left two decades later?

What is a Nationalist? He can simply be someone who loves his homeland, but it has come to mean much more than that. A dictionary definition is 'someone who desires political independence for his nation'. That too may sound reasonably simple, but it leaves open for debate which nation that might be, and what, indeed, is a nation. Disputes over these questions have led to European wars and frequent local conflicts.

It is not too difficult to see why many in Ireland have become strongly Nationalist in that sense. As an island it has distinct boundaries, has had for centuries a settled population who speak the same language and share the Christian religion, and have generally had a sense of their own identity, distinct from their immediate neighbours. But not all on the island have seen that identity as sufficiently distinct to constitute a nation, entitled to claim independence for the whole island.

Growing up in Unionist Lisburn I had no doubt that I lived in Ireland, and that I was Irish. That did not mean I was not British, but during the Second World War our great hero was not the Englishman Winston Churchill, but General Montgomery, because he was Irish, or at least we could claim he was Irish via his Donegal forebears.

But politics in Northern Ireland were, and still are, confined within the Unionist-Nationalist confrontation. To be Nationalist meant to be against partition and for the removal of Northern Ireland from the United Kingdom, and its incorporation into an all-Ireland Republic, because that was right, and partition was wrong. That unity could come only with the consent of Unionists, or at least of a majority in the North, had been the official line since Lemass, but that was a recognition of a practical difficulty, not a modification of the Nationalist insistence that partition was morally wrong, and that reunification was, ultimately, the only possible solution.

I was never a Nationalist in that narrow meaning. Neither was I a Unionist, for a Unionist was, and still is, someone who believes in and strongly supports the idea and ideals of the Union; he believes that 'Ulster is British' is not just a statement of fact, but an assertion of a fundamental truth. That is, that he is part of the British nation, and has a right to live within the British state, and for his home territory to be part of it.

It is possible to subscribe to neither of those viewpoints – rejecting one does not mean you embrace the other. Writing as a journalist in Dublin, for readers who were politically Nationalist, it was patently more useful and relevant for me to examine and criticise the ways in which the Nationalist interpretation of the problem was flawed, and was a factor in perpetuating that problem. (I had, when in Belfast, dealt mainly in criticism of Unionism.)

Unfortunately, so strongly have these contending political stances held sway over minds in the two parts of the island that it has been almost impossible for anyone to criticise one without being promptly, and wrongly, labelled as the other.

A besetting sin, North and South, is to side-step the argument by labelling the man. Thus it has been easier over the years to dismiss Conor Cruise O'Brien as Unionist, and so not be troubled by his devastating analysis of Irish Nationalism. So too it was easier to dismiss the dissenting voice in editorial conferences, or in *The Irish Times'* pages, as Unionist, than to try to understand the argument.

I did not leave Ireland when I left Dublin and moved back North. I still have my Irish passport, I still look on Dublin as my home, as much as, if not more than, Belfast. My National Gallery is in Merrion Square, not Trafalgar, and my National Museum in Kildare Street, not Bloomsbury (though it is good to have such fine second strings in those two places).